Circular Walks

in the

South Hams

Exploring South Devon

Simone Stanbrook–Byrne

and

James Clancy

CULM VALLEY PUBLISHING

Published by:
Culm Valley Publishing Ltd
Culmcott House
Mill Street, Uffculme
Cullompton, Devon
EX15 3AT, UK
Tel / fax: +44(0)1884 849085
E-mail: info@culmvalleypublishing.co.uk
Website: www.culmvalleypublishing.co.uk

While every effort has been made to ensure the accuracy of the information contained in
this book, the publisher and authors accepts no liability for incorrect information
regarding public footpaths and rights of way. Neither Culm Valley Publishing Ltd nor the
authors shall be liable for any damages whatsoever arising in any way from the use of or
inability to use this book, or any material contained within it, or from any action or
decision taken as a result of using this book. Follow the country code.

First published 2014

ISBN 978-1-907942-11-2 paperback

British Library Cataloguing-in-Publication Data
A catalogue record for this book is available from the British Library

Typeset by Culm Valley Publishing Ltd

Printed and bound by:
Ashford Colour Press Ltd, Gosport, Hants PO13 0FW

Front cover image: Sunshine and shadows across the River Dart (Walk 4)
Back cover image: Approaching Beenleigh Brook (Walk 9)

All images used in this book are available as cards and prints from Culm Valley Publishing

Contents

4

Introduction

Writing this walking guide has been very enjoyable. We've walked through fabulous views, found hidden paths, enjoyed country inns with open fires or sunny gardens, discovered new places and rediscovered some old ones.

On any walk common sense must prevail: be properly shod and take care where you put your feet; be prepared for any kind of weather; take food and first aid supplies with you and make sure someone knows where you're going. Mobile phones are often useless in the middle of nowhere.

We feel it's important that you take the **correct OS map** with you plus a **compass** (where advised) and are conversant with their use. Our sketch maps are precisely that – sketches – and are for rough guidance only and not necessarily to scale.

You know you've had a good day's walking when you get home safely at the end of it.

Follow the countryside code:
www.naturalengland.org.uk/ourwork/enjoying/countrysidecode/

Our grateful thanks to:

The volunteers of Froward Point and Prawle Point Coastwatch Stations for some fascinating insights and replenishing our water bottles

Brian and Jenny Willan

Nic and Tony

The Fisherman's Cot, Bickleigh, nr Tiverton – a proofreading location with a fabulous view

Disciaimer

Points that should be borne in mind on any route:

Public footpaths can be legally re-routed from the path shown on the map. In such cases they are usually clearly signposted. Where this has happened before the time of writing it has been noted in the text.

Most public footpaths are on private land. Please respect this.

Don't be surprised to find livestock grazing on public footpaths – and treat all animals with caution and respect.

If a field is planted with crops across a footpath, provision is usually made around the edge of the field.

Landmarks can change: trees and hedges may disappear; streams can dry up in warm weather or flood after heavy rain; stiles turn into gates and vice versa; fences appear where previously there was no boundary. Even views are different as the seasons progress. In such cases a modicum of common sense must be exercised – in conjunction with the OS map.

Public footpaths are at times blocked by barbed wire etc. Should this render the route impassable find the shortest detour around that section.

Please leave gates as you find them and if you have to climb them do so at the hinge end where it's stronger.

Exercise caution on wet stiles – they can be extremely slippery.

Take all your rubbish with you, please don't damage anything during the walk and please don't pick plants.

Please keep your dogs under proper control.

We hope that you enjoy these walks without mishap, but urge you to exercise common sense at all times. Neither the authors nor Culm Valley Publishing Ltd accepts responsibility for any misadventure that may occur during, or arise from, these walks and suggested routes.

Walk Locations

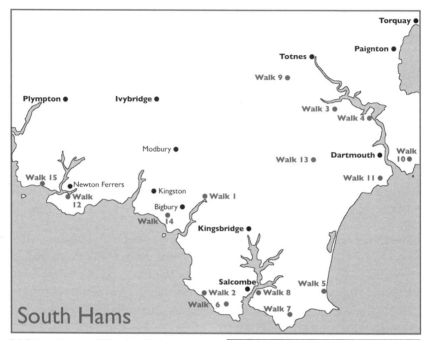

South Hams

Walk 1   **Aveton Gifford & Bigbury**

Walk 2   **Bolberry Down & Soar Mill Cove**

Walk 3   **Cornworthy & Tuckenhay**

Walk 4   **Dittisham & Old Mill Creek**

Walk 5   **Hallsands & Start Point**

Walk 6   **Salcombe Estuary & Bolt Head**

Walk 7   **East Prawle & Prawle Point**

Walk 8   **East Portlemouth**

Walk 9   **Harberton**

Walk 10   **Kingswear**

Walk 11   **Little Dartmouth**

Walk 12   **Noss Mayo**

Walk 13   **Blackawton**

Walk 14   **Ringmore & Kingston**

Walk 15   **Wembury & the River Yealm**

Wayside stall (Walk 9)

Walk 1

Aveton Gifford & Bigbury

Distance: 4¼ miles / 6.8km

*A walk of glorious views, superb birdwatching and a path for the inebriated. In the raw months at the start of the year the route is bejewelled by snowdrops – enjoy them without picking please! The finishing stretch, descending towards the estuary, is a real treat; listen for the haunting cry of curlew and the rhythmic pulse of mute swans in flight. As it's tidal you **must** check the tide times. It can be very wet in places so wellies are a good idea and there are a few uphill stretches.*

Map: OS Explorer OL20, South Devon, Brixham to Newton Ferrers 1:25 000

Start point: Car park near roundabout on edge of Aveton Gifford. Grid ref: SX692472. Nearby postcode: TQ7 4JL

Directions to start: Aveton Gifford is situated in South Devon on the A379

Parking: Car park as per start point above

Public Transport: Aveton Gifford is served by buses from the following operators: First in Devon & Cornwall and Plymouth Citybus. The nearest railway station is Ivybridge

Refreshments: Fisherman's Rest, Aveton Gifford, 01548 550284; the village shop for chocolate supplies, 01548 550996

Toilets: Near Aveton Gifford post office and shop in centre of village

Nearby places to stay: Court Barton Farm, Aveton Gifford, 01548 550312

Nearby places of interest: Cookworthy Museum, 108 Fore Street, Kingsbridge, 01548 853235; South Devon Chilli Farm, Wigford Cross, Loddiswell, 01548 550782

Possible birds include: Blackbird, blue tit, buzzard, carrion crow, chaffinch, chiffchaff, curlew, dunnock, goldfinch, great tit, green woodpecker, greenshank, grey heron, gulls, jackdaw, little egret, magpie, mallard, mute swan, oystercatcher, pheasant, shelduck, skylark, woodpigeon, wren, yellow wagtail, yellowhammer

Authors' tip: If you are in anyway ornithologically-minded ensure you take binoculars on this walk. The estuary habitat supports a variety of birds

Note: Be aware: this walk ends along a tidal road which is impassable at times, so check the tide details on the website (www.aveton-gifford.co.uk/local-info/weather-tides-surf/) before starting out and allow yourself enough time to cover the distance so that you are finishing the walk well away from the time of high tide

Leave the car park at its bottom corner, where a ford crosses the lane. Turn right along the lane, the main body of the River Avon is beyond the grass to your left. Follow the lane for 100m to reach a cottage on the right

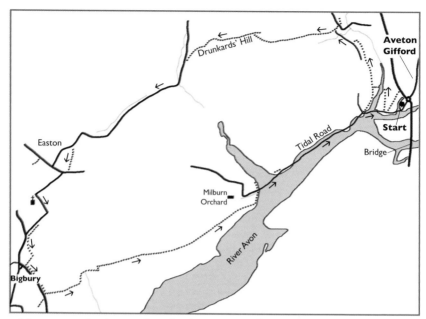

with two nearby footpaths. The first, going sharply back on yourself, you don't need. Take the second path, just beyond the wall surrounding the cottage, heading right across a field at 90° to the lane. Follow this path as the arrow directs to arrive at a boardwalk in just over 100m. Here go left, hop across the stepping stones and continue beyond them to an obvious three-way fingerpost. Keep straight on, entering under trees where the

Initial views of the River Avon from the tidal road

Drunkards' Hill

path turns right to follow a fence on the left. The clear, yellow-arrowed path takes you over two stiles before climbing up to a third beyond which steps rise up to a surfaced track.

Go right at the top of the steps along the track for about 150m. At the brow of a gentle rise you find a footpath going left on the Avon Estuary Walk, its symbol is a heron. Follow the direction of the fingerpost, up steps, over a stile and through the field beyond with rising ground to your right and the boundary to your left. When the boundary on the left swings sharp left a yellow arrow on the corner post directs you straight across the field, uphill. Pause as you climb to enjoy the views behind.

 This line brings you to another arrowed post from which you continue, now with a hedge to your left again and still in the same field. In the top corner turn right with the boundary to reach a stile a few metres further along. Cross this and bear right across the field to a substantial stile in the corner; note the intriguing, ivy-clad ruins over to your left. At the stile you reach the curiously named Drunkards' Hill, go left along this old byway pondering the origins of the name – it's been called this since at least the mid 19thC.

Follow Drunkards' Hill until it deposits you on the lane, then turn left and follow the lane through a pretty hamlet, passing Foxhole Cottage. Climb rather breathily onwards, as the lane trudges uphill for almost ½ mile until you pass Glebe Barn and Old Glebe. A few bends bring you to

Countryside views from Drunkards' Hill

the buildings of Easton and opposite its main entrance a footpath goes left off the lane, over a stile and into a field. Cross the field towards the tallest telegraph pole in the top boundary, 150m away, beneath which a lovely, old fashioned, metal kissing gate brings you out to the lane.

Go right and in about 50m fork left at Bowls Cross, heading for Bigbury. In 220m the lane bends left and you soon pass the rather imposing gateposts of the church, their grandeur softened by ferns and wall pennywort. After a sharp right bend and opposite the main entrance of Bigbury Court you find a footpath going left off the lane, up stone steps to a fingerpost.

At the top of the steps ignore the direction of the fingerpost as the path has been unofficially re-routed. Instead, follow the right-hand boundary round the field, entering a second field through a gap not far from houses (to the right). Continue beside the right-hand boundary in this second field, following the perimeter for 500m from the steps until you reach access on to the lane beside a substantial three-way fingerpost.

Here, stay in the field and go left, rejoining the Avon Estuary Walk signed towards Milburn Orchard, 1½ miles away. This clear path crosses the field to reach a stile with a well-trodden path beyond – you will have glimpses of the estuary down to your right. Follow the path as it winds into the trees of Doctor's Wood. It emerges from the trees and rises up to a wooden kissing gate. After this turn left and follow the fence on your left,

Aveton Gifford

A settlement since prehistoric times, Aveton Gifford derives its name from three sources: the River Avon on which it lies, the Celtic word 'ton' meaning town and the Giffard family who held the manor here from the late 11thC, Walter Giffard arriving in England with William the Conqueror. The interesting  church dates back to the 13thC but sadly the wonderful Early English architecture suffered massive damage during WWII. It was subsequently rebuilt, with the retention of some of its earlier architectural features, although the tower had to be reconstructed again in 1970. The unusual tidal road to the village was once a cart track serving nearby farms, a limekiln and a mill. It was called the 'Stakes Road' for obvious reasons. At low tide horses could wade across and people used stepping stones. Once the road was constructed with proper drainage it made for easier passage.

Stepping stones

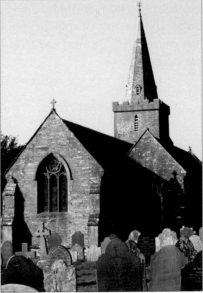

St Lawrence Bigbury

walking high above the estuary. When the fence swings sharp left keep straight ahead to gates about 50m away.

Go through the most right-hand of the gates (at the time of writing it was only part-constructed but we think it will grow up to be a kissing gate). Beyond here you start to descend towards the estuary. Another kissing gate and the view opens up even more, the walking is wonderful along this lofty path. As the left-hand hedge bends left keep straight ahead, descending across the field, estuary down to your right and Aveton Gifford with its bridge way off in the distance.

This line brings you to a stile, continue beyond it as before; if your left leg shorter than the right you'll feel better on this stretch! Keep following the well-trodden path over stiles until you reach one beneath a tree with a slithery path beyond it leading to steps down to the edge of the estuary. Hopefully the tide is right and you can skirt across the back of the mud, passing attractive water gardens on your left, to reach a fingerpost by an information board. Go through the gate and turn right along the tidal road, trying not to dwell overly on any *Woman in Black*; there is no Eel Marsh House hereabouts but over to your left you will see the old limekiln. As you continue, enjoying myriad birds, you'll be walking under the shadow of cliffs to your left, trees clinging on precariously. In just over 1km (0.7 miles) you'll find yourself back at the entrance to your car park.

Descending to the River Avon with Aveton Gifford in the background

Bolberry Down & Soar Mill Cove
Distance: 3½ miles / 5.4km

One of our favourite sections of coastline, this is a superb spot and Soar Mill Cove itself is a delightful place for a paddle. The first half of the walk explores attractive farmland, quiet lanes and the tranquil valley behind the coast, while the jewel in the walk's crown, the coastal stretch, comes later. Bolberry Down has known human activity for millennia, with tools being unearthed that date back to 1500BC. It's a good area for birdwatching, plus wild flowers and butterflies in summer. There is one steep climb out of the cove but otherwise it's a fairly gentle walk.

Map: OS Explorer OL20, South Devon, Brixham to Newton Ferrers 1:25 000

Start point: Bolberry Down. Grid ref: SX688385. Nearest postcode (for Port Light Inn):TQ7 3DY

Directions to start: Bolberry Down is south of Malborough off the A381

Parking: National Trust car park at start

Public Transport: No bus service. Nearest railway station is Ivybridge

Refreshments: Port Light Inn, 01548 561384; Soar Mill Cove Hotel, 01548 561566

Toilets: None en route unless using refreshment stops

Nearby places to stay: Port Light Inn, 01548 561384; Soar Mill Cove Hotel, 01548 561566

Nearby places of interest: The Wreck Room in Salcombe Maritime Museum, Market St, 01548 843080

Possible birds include: Blackbird, blue tit, buzzard, carrion crown, cormorant, goldfinch, great tit, gulls, house sparrow, kestrel, linnet, magpie, meadow pipit, peregrine, raven, shag, skylark, stonechat, swallow, wheatear, whitethroat, willow warbler, woodpigeon, wren, yellowhammer

Authors' tip: If the weather is conducive take towels and enjoy a paddle at Soar Mill Cove. If you aren't covered in mud and perhaps have something to celebrate you could do so in Soar Mill Cove Hotel's Bollinger Bar

Start by savouring the panorama from the car park and then leave it along the lane by which you drove in, passing the tall radio mast in the field to the right. Gateway views on the left permit glimpses along the coast towards Bigbury and Burgh Island with its white Art Deco hotel. In about 350m you find a green lane, Jacob's Lane, on the right. Take this. In 650m you reach a footpath going right through a gate to cross the land of

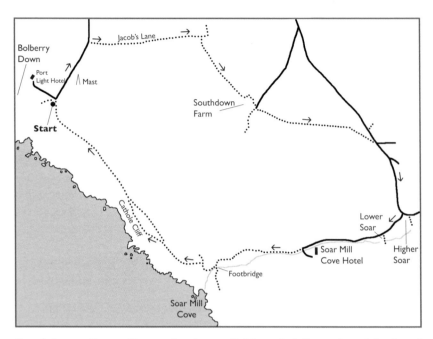

Southdown Farm. Enter the large field and follow the right-hand boundary, glancing behind to the left where you'll see the distinctive shape of Malborough Church. At the end of the field keep ahead between hedges, approaching farm buildings.

When you arrive at a surfaced track go diagonally left across it, as the fingerpost directs, to continue on the arrowed footpath beyond. A gate leads to a path beside a National Trust hut and parking area; follow the frequent yellow arrows beyond here, the buildings of Southdown Farm over to your right. You soon reach a three-way fingerpost by steps leading down to the farm drive. Go straight across, clambering over a stone stile to join the footpath opposite. Walk ahead through the field along the line of the right-hand boundary in which occasional gaps afford lovely valley views. Also look out for the craggy profile of a petrified giant poodle.

About 200m along this boundary you'll see a fingerpost directing you obliquely left across the field, so strike away from the hedge towards another fingerpost that you can see in the distance. Salcombe can also be seen way ahead. At the fingerpost pass through the boundary and continue for almost 100m until you reach a stepped stile descending to the lane – mind how you fall down it.

Turn right along the lane, ignoring both an immediate left turn and then a left fork in just over 100m. Keep on the lane signed for Soar Mill Cove Hotel. You pass the attractive buildings of Lower and Higher Soar with their bright red letterbox. Keep heading for the hotel, passing The Olde Cottage and Hazel Tor Barn on your left. The lane leads you past the beach car park above the hotel and soon after that the main drive into the hotel. Here you'll find a footpath gate ahead of you to the right, pass through and follow the yellow-arrowed path downhill towards the cove. This is a lovely stretch of grassy walking, redolent of 'Dartmoor by the sea'.

Keep heading downhill, the path becomes stony at intervals but is always unmissable, until you arrive at the idyllic cove. Relish the area. Paddle.

When you've had enough pick up the acorn-waymarked coast path, indicated on a fingerpost behind the beach, heading for Bolberry and Bolt Tail. Follow the path away from the cove, sea to your left. You can see the poodle again from here though it's not her best side. A short distance from the cove is a three-way fingerpost with a badge showing grid ref SX697377; follow the leftwards coast path with the sea to your left and ignore the more inland, lower route.

Looking back towards Soar Mill Cove Hotel

Wrecks

Over the centuries the seas off the South Devon coast have proved treacherous for many ships and the area has been littered with wrecks and treasure; in the 1990s a diving team discovered gold from the wreck of a 17thC trading ship armed with cannon. Bronze Age artefacts have also been found. One notable ship was a 216ft (66m) long, full-rigged tea clipper called The Hallow E'en. She was built in 1820 in Greenwich, a sister ship to Blackadder. Renowned for speed, during the winter of 1874–5 The Hallow E'en sailed from Shanghai to London in a record 91 days. In 1887 she came to grief in Soar Mill Cove whilst importing a cargo of 1600 tons of tea from Fuzhou in China. There was, reputedly, a wall of tea on the beach almost 3m high. The wreck now lies in 11m of water.

Quite a breathy climb lies ahead but the views make it all worthwhile. Pause to glance back, it's good there too, and partake of occasional well-placed benches. Eventually you reach a particularly finely-placed bench, engraved 'MKW' on its cove side; a good place to perch and feel well-pleased with the fact that you bothered. Enjoy the glorious coastal scenery, the play of light on the sea and survey the route that you've just travelled, back up the valley past Soar Mill Cove Hotel and across to Southdown Farm. You can see from here how unobtrusive the hotel is.

The inviting beach at Soar Mill Cove

Evening sunlight from the coast path

Admiring the views over Soar Mill Cove

Pandora enjoys the coast views

Once refreshed continue on the coast path and soon the radio mast at Bolberry comes into sight again. You have good views in all directions along this stretch above Cathole Cliff. You may also encounter rather adorable (and peaceable) Highland Cattle who are helping out with the habitat management along this stretch. The path leads you past an information board about the area before depositing you back in the car park from whence you started.

Highland Cattle sometimes graze above Cathole Cliff

Walk 3
Cornworthy & Tuckenhay
Distance: 5.6 miles / 9km

Redolent of an age long-gone, when 'traffic' consisted solely of drovers, walkers and horseriders, Devon's 'green lanes' enable us to follow in the footsteps of ancestors who used these old ways to get to church, to market and to generally go about their daily business. This walk explores part of a network of rather romantic tracks and incorporates a section of the John Musgrave Heritage Trail, John Musgrave being a former chairman of the South Devon Group of the Ramblers' Association. Lovely at any time of year, the birdwatching is rewarding along the section by Bow Creek and in autumn the colours are spectacular. Listen out for the toot of trains on the Dartmouth Steam Railway and the haunting cry of curlew along the creek, a sound which should be bottled. The route can be muddy in places, be well-booted.

Map: OS Explorer OL20, South Devon, Brixham to Newton Ferrers 1:25 000

Start point: At the road junction in Cornworthy near the Parish Church of St. Peter. Grid ref: SX829555. Postcode: TQ9 7ES

Directions to start: Cornworthy is signed off the A381 just beyond Totnes

Parking: Park on street, please exercise courtesy towards residents

Public Transport: Very limited buses details from www.travelinesw.com. The nearest train station is Totnes

Refreshments: The Maltsters Arms, Tuckenhay, 01803 732350; Hunters Lodge Inn, Cornworthy, 01803 732204 (up for sale at time of writing)

Toilets: None en route unless using inns

Nearby places to stay: Kerswell Farm, Cornworthy, 01803 732013; The Maltsters Arms, Tuckenhay, 01803 732350

Nearby places of interest: Dartmouth Castle, Castle Road, Dartmouth, 01803 833588 or 839618; Totnes Castle, 01803 864406

Possible birds include: Black swan, blackbird, blue tit, bullfinch, buzzard, Canada goose, chaffinch, cormorant, carrion crow, curlew, dipper, fieldfare, goldfinch, great tit, grey wagtail, gulls, heron, jackdaw, jay, long-tailed tit, magpie, mallard, marsh tit, moorhen, mute swan, pied wagtail, redwing, robin, shelduck, song thrush, sparrowhawk, swallow, swift, woodpigeon, wren

Authors' tip: Allow time to explore Cornworthy and seek out the information board beside the entrance to Cornworthy Court. From this point look between the houses across to the ruins on the hillside opposite. These are the remains of the 15thC gatehouse to a 13thC Augustinian priory, in use until 1536. The ruins can be accessed off the lane adjacent to them

---

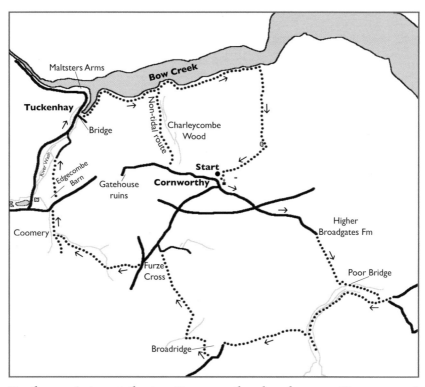

On the road sign at the junction near the church you will see several footpath arrows: The John Musgrave Heritage Trail, the Dart Valley Trail and Cornworthy Circular Walks. Follow the lane signposted towards East Cornworthy and Dittisham, climbing steadily to reach Longland Cross in about 350m. Here keep straight ahead, signed towards Broadgates and an unmetalled road. There are entrance gates on the right here stating 'Parva Domus, Magna Quies ('small house, great peace') and as you approach Higher Broadgates Farm along this lane the expansive, undulating hillside to the right undoubtedly does afford a sense of wellbeing to those who overlook the valley. The lane begins to descend and by the time you pass Higher Broadgates Farm it's rough underfoot. Keep on the track past the buildings, a fingerpost indicates that you're heading along Broadgates Lane towards Dittisham, 2 miles away.

This lovely, if potentially muddy, green lane crosses Barberry Water at the 19thC Poor Bridge, just over ½ km from the farm. You reach a crossing

St. Peter's Church, Cornworthy

track at a three-way fingerpost; go right here towards Broadridge, still following a green lane, its banks decorated with male and hart's tongue ferns and red campion. Gateway views invite a break for some chocolate and a photo, then continue on the track, crossing another bridge (ignore a bridleway going left) and climbing on and on. The track eventually emerges from the trees after which you can pause for breath and admire the views behind towards Galmpton on the other side of the Dart Valley. About 700m from the bridge you arrive at Broadridge House, go left on the lane and follow it around the environs of the house until, just beyond

Just beyond Poor Bridge

Tuckenhay

Strolling through this tranquil and idyllic place it's hard to imagine the industrial buzz which pervaded the area during the 19thC and for the first half of the 20thC. The river was a good source of water power for industry and enabled easy transportation. The village derives its name from Abraham Tucker who  moved his family's hemp and flax processing business here around the end of the 18thC, and the buildings of this subsequently became the extensive paper mill which supplied high quality paper for use by artists, in bank notes and for royal proclamations. There were many forms of industry hereabouts including lime kilns and quarries and the river bustled with shipping; barges and tall ships calling at its quays. Cast your mind back and imagine these times.....before the creek silted up and the hubbub ceased, leaving the birds and pleasure boats we see today and with occasional cottage names reminiscent of the industrial past. More recent history involves The Maltsters Arms, which was owned by 'colourful' TV chef Keith Floyd during the 1990s.

the entrance to Broadridge Farm, you find a fingerpost directing you off the lane.

Take this through the field, keeping the hedge on your right with Lower Tideford Farm on the hillside ahead of you. The track soon bends right and goes down to a gate. Beyond this bear left as shown by the arrow, going steeply down the field to an arrowed post in the boundary. This points you on to a sunken path going down the side of the field with the fence to your right. Another arrowed post directs you right, down to a diminutive footbridge. Go through a gate beyond this and bear obliquely right up the next field to a gate in the boundary, across to the right is a wind turbine and the buildings of Broadridge which you passed earlier. At the gate go through and turn left, following the left boundary up the field. There are gorgeous views right (north east) towards Windmill Hill Clump, distinctive in the distance; behind to the right are sea views.

At the top of the field go left and immediately right, continuing in the same direction but now with the hedge on your right. The panorama ahead is superb; the southern range of Dartmoor in the distance stretches from west to east. Closer to hand you may spot wild pansies, try not to tread on them. Keep ahead through another field, Tuckenhay with its church is ahead, and soon the path emerges on to the drive of Southills Farm. Go left away from the buildings to reach the lane within 100m, then go left along the lane. In 150m, at Furze Cross, you find a grassy triangle at the far end of which a fingerpost points right off the lane beside the drive to Kerswell Farmhouse. Go through the gate into the field and follow the path across it, this line brings you alongside a row of trees, gradually descending to the far side of the field where you find a

Superb countryside en route

combination of stiles and a plank bridge to lead you into the next field. Walk through this following the line of the right-hand boundary with rising ground to the left.

At the end of the field enter another and keep beside the boundary to reach a tucked-away gate beneath trees. Beyond here follow a broad track, stream to the right, into a more open area. Keep ahead on the track, passing a series of barns on the left, to arrive at the thatched and idyllic-looking Coomery Farm. Turn right. In 200m you reach a lane, turn right again, watching for cars, and within 100m you find the entrance to Edgecombe Barn on the left. Turn in here and keep ahead on the signed

The attractive waterside community of Tuckenhay

unmetalled road which climbs uphill. As the track levels you find (if it hasn't fully decomposed) a very organic bench, originally inviting passers-by to 'rest and be thankful'. By the time we arrived it said 't and be thankful' – even more appealing really. If it hasn't mouldered away appreciate it, then continue downhill until you reach the lane in Tuckenhay. Continue past the old mill buildings, now holiday homes, continuing left downhill with the lane past the mill's main entrance and across the River Wash until you reach Coronation Cross. Turn right here along the lane to Tuckenhay Bridge, which spans the river on your right. Here the walk goes across the bridge, but first you may wish to keep ahead for about 250m to sample the delights of The Maltsters Arms, a well-situated inn that's like a bird hide with a bar and restaurant.

Back on the route, cross Tuckenhay Bridge and in a few metres, just before the lane swings right, go left on the public footpath, ignoring the track ahead. This path follows the banks of Bow Creek to your left, looking across at creek-side houses with their suspended boats; a lovely, sylvan stretch of walking. A kissing gate leads into a field, keep going round the perimeter, creek to the left, following the well-arrowed path until, about ½ mile from leaving the lane, you reach a three-way fingerpost.

Here the route continues ahead on the 'tidal route' but if you're walking at times of very high tide you may need to take the shorter option right, back to Cornworthy, from ** below.

Alongside Bow Creek

For the longer, tidal route go left across the stile and follow the clear path beside the creek; this is our favourite bit. The path soon ducks under trees and goes up steps. Keep going, it's a very clear route through successive patches of woodland and open areas, the creek always to your left. About 600m from the fingerpost the path gets very close to the creek, its banks softened by the tiny, lush leaves of 'mind your own business'. Beyond this a stile leads into a delightful, creek-lapped field, a place that tempts the walker to sit awhile and observe, with a well-placed bench and a big chunk of oak tree, sawn into three seats rather reminiscent of the Isle of Man symbol.

Leaving Bow Creek for Cornworthy

At the far end of the field a yellow arrow points right away from the creek, but first take a moment to study the tree beside the gate, at high tide its fingers dip into the saltwater which has had an odd effect on the bark. Turn right within the field and walk uphill, keeping the boundary to your left and glancing back across the hillside as you go. At the top continue on the track, climbing and bending about, as arrows direct, until, after a right bend, the church tower in Cornworthy beckons. You arrive in the yard of Cornworthy Court. Arrows direct you to bear left through the yard, round the corner of the house and away from the farm on a track below the church. This quickly leads out to the lane, close to the point from whence you started.

**Shorter, non-tidal route:
From the three-way fingerpost go right on the clear track, arrows directing you away from the creek to soon enter a field. Keep ahead with the boundary to your left and a steep slope up to the right. In about 100m you have the option to go left into Charleycombe Wood, planted in 1999 as part of the Woodland Trust's 'Woodland on your Doorstep' project. In this area follow the path across a footbridge, bearing right after the bridge with a stream to your right. Ignore the next bridge to the right and keep on to a further bridge, after which a path leads steeply up to a gate, beyond which it rejoins the track. Go left, passing cottages on the outskirts of Cornworthy, until you reach the lane through the village. Turn left back towards the church and your start point.

Walk 4
Dittisham & Old Mill Creek
Distance: 4¾ miles / 7.6km

A beautiful inland walk above the River Dart and Old Mill Creek. Enjoy field paths with glorious views, enticing woodland tracks and idyllic cottages; listen out for the romantic chuff of occasional steam trains across the river and round it off with a visit to one of the lovely Dittisham pubs or café. The walk has a few hills to warm you up and there are some wet areas so walking boots are a good idea.

Map: OS Explorer OL20, South Devon, Brixham to Newton Ferrers 1:25 000

Start point: The Level Car Park, The Level, Dittisham. Grid ref: SX863547. Postcode: TQ6 0ES

Directions to start: Dittisham is a village on the west bank of the River Dart, 2 miles upstream of Dartmouth. It can be accessed via lanes from the A381

Parking: The Level Car Park

Public Transport: No buses call at Dittisham but there is a ferry service across the River Dart from Greenway which is a lovely way to arrive. Bus operator AC1 calls at Greenway. Timetables available online at www.travelinesw.com. Nearest railway station is Totnes

Refreshments: Anchorstone Café, Manor Street, Dittisham, 01803 722365; Ferry Boat Inn, Manor Street, Dittisham, 01803 722368; Red Lion Inn, The Level, Dittisham, 01803 722235

Toilets: None en route, but there are public toilets in Dittisham at Ham Lane Car Park (TQ6 0HB)

Nearby places to stay: Cott Farm B&B, Dittisham, 01803 722259; Downton Lodge Country Guest House, Dittisham, 01803 722249

Nearby places of interest: Greenway (NT), Greenway Road, Galmpton, 01803 842382; Sharpham Vineyard, Ashprington, 01803 732203

Possible birds include: Black swan, buzzard, carrion crow, grey heron, grey wagtail, great spotted woodpecker, gulls, jay, kingfisher, little egret, mute swan, pheasant, pied wagtail, raven, woodpigeon, wren

Authors' tip: Consider taking the ferry from Dittisham to Greenway to visit Agatha Christie's house. This was a summer retreat for the much-loved author from 1938 until her death in 1976

Leave the car park and go left along the lane, climbing gently and bending left. As it goes sharp left down Manor Street keep ahead along Rectory Lane, passing The White House on your left. This is a public footpath to Dartmouth and part of the Dart Valley Trail (from time to time

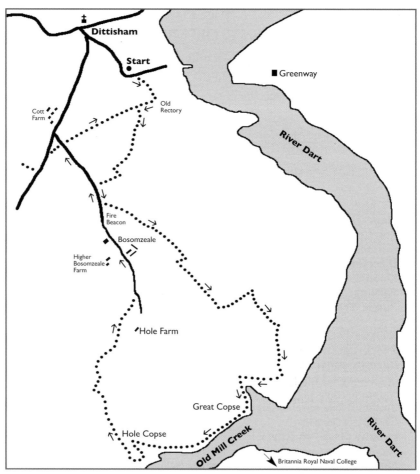

you'll see the white arrow on blue background). Just before the Old Rectory go right on a signposted footpath off the lane, which in a few metres rises to bring you to a broad crossing track. Go right on this through the kissing gate, to continue up the rising track for about 100m to where a footpath leaves the track, going left over a V-shaped stile and into a field.

Climb the field with the hedge to your right, relishing the superb views expanding to your left as you climb. Across the river you can see Agatha Christie's Greenway, now owned by the National Trust. The path passes above a majestic oak, bracing itself against gravity on the sloping field below, and reaches a stile in the top corner. Continue in the same direction through another three fields, keeping the boundary to your right. In the third field keep by the boundary as it swings left then right again to reach the lane.

Turn left on the lane, Fire Beacon Hill, and you will see the beacon firebasket ahead of you on a pole; originally this site formed part of the chain of beacons used to warn of the approaching Spanish Armada in 1588. Before you reach the beacon go left off the lane on a permissive footpath to Old Mill Creek, passing an information board about Raleigh's River Dart just as you enter the field. Follow the track through the field, along the line of the right-hand boundary. In clear weather from this elevated spot you have views left across Torbay and beyond along the coast of East Devon towards Dorset. At the end of the field continue through the next, still along the line of the right-hand hedge.

At the end of this field keep ahead through the gate into the next field and cross it, bearing slightly right towards the far boundary to find a gate with the Dart Valley Trail arrow (make sure you get the arrowed gate). As you go you'll see the day mark tower dominating the hill in the distance (see feature on the Kingswear walk). Once in the next field follow the line of the left-hand hedge with valley views to your right. As you proceed the River Dart comes into view again and the red brick rear

The beautiful River Dart

Hermitage Castle

Hermitage Castle, sometimes referred to as Old Mill castle, was rebuilt in the 19thC on the site of an earlier building, as a folly for the Seale family. The Seales were Dartmouth merchants who were first recorded in the area in the early 15thC and who took up residence here from Jersey in 1720. They were  substantial landowners and the grounds of their mansion, Mount Boone, extended down to the banks of Old Mill Creek. The castle is Grade II listed and has undergone restoration in recent years, voluntary work being carried out by cadets from the Royal Naval College at Dartmouth.

elevation of the Britannia Royal Naval College in Dartmouth. The cluster of houses clinging to the hillside ahead is Kingswear, just across the estuary. To your right are the houses of Townstal and way over to the right you can see the water tower at Jawbones, above Dartmouth.

At the end of the field a two-way fingerpost directs you left along a track, dropping downhill and passing under trees. Keep your eyes peeled for another arrow in about 250m directing you right off the track and down to a gate. Go through here and follow the track beyond; this is fenced from the field to your right and through the hedge to your left are valley views across Klingate Covert to a shipyard, the gable end of a red brick building proudly displaying 'Philip & Son Ltd. Shipbuilders & Engineers Estd. 1858'.

The path winds a bit, goes down, then up, then down again. Keep with it, you have no choice. As you proceed more views of the Dart reveal themselves, it's often busy with boats and if the light and weather are right the opposite hillside becomes a playground for racing cloud shadows. Old Mill Creek comes into view ahead and below you. Eventually the path deposits you at a small metal gate with an arrow. Go through here, crossing a short track and heading downhill across the field in the direction of the arrow towards another small gate, the water is to your left. Look behind over your left shoulder here, across the Dart; if you're lucky you may catch sight of one of the steam trains chugging along the line out of Kingswear. A path beyond the gate leads you down towards the creek, Sandquay Wood cladding the valley-side beyond. Another metal gate leads into the conifer plantation of Great Copse. In here go left down wooden-edged steps which lead into an open area, a pond on your right and the creek on your left. Keep ahead, looking out for kingfishers, and follow the clear track beside the creek. A path comes down to join you from the right, keep going and soon you enter the pine-fragranced Hole Copse; a lovely stretch of needle-softened walking is ahead of you with glimpses through the trees on your left of Hermitage

Looking over Noss Marina and Philip & Son Shipbuilders

Castle across the creek. If there is a breeze pause and look up; above their immobile trunks these incredibly tall, graceful pine trees dance against the sky. The track starts to climb and bends left to cross a verdant area of babbling waterfalls. Keep climbing as the track bends about until you reach a kissing gate with a three-way fingerpost and an information board beyond.

Left is to the Old Mill Creek Inn but, alas, your way lies to the right, along Lapthorne Lane – one of Devon's lovely green lanes which can be quite wet underfoot. Follow Lapthorne Lane for more than 500m until you reach a fingerpost. Here the track continues on to Lapthorne Farm without you as you now go right along a bridleway, still part of the Dart

Valley Trail. This climbs steadily to a wooden gate, continue beyond it on the hedged track as it eventually bends right and arrives at a broad meeting of gates, just under 250m from leaving Lapthorne Lane. Don't be tempted into any fields but keep ahead as the track continues until it brings you through a gate into an open field with good views to the right across the Dart to the day mark tower. Cross the field in the direction of the arrow, bearing slightly left to the far corner where you'll find a gate. Pass through and join a surfaced track beyond, turn left along this away from Hole Farm.

You pass attractive barn conversions on the right and the wonderfully-named Higher Bosomzeale Farm on the left. Keep ahead, passing the fire beacon you saw earlier followed by two footpaths on the right, both of which you've already walked. Keep on the lane as distant views of Dartmoor appear (you'll need a clear day to appreciate this), birthplace of the river which is ahead of you and closer to hand. 550m from the beacon you reach a crossing footpath, go right here along a stony track which offers good views to the left. The track descends past a stile which you negotiated earlier; keep ahead on the track and from here you are retracing your steps down to the Old Rectory, then turning left along the lane to follow the road ahead until you arrive back at the car park.

Lovely tree on footpath by Old Mill Creek

Walk 5

Hallsands & Start Point

Distance: 4¾ miles / 7.6km

Superb coastal walking with big skies, expansive sea views and some fascinating history to start you off. You have a chance of seeing seals basking on the rocks and we saw more stonechats on this walk than on any other – listen for their 'chinking' call, it sounds like pebbles being tapped together. You may also be treated to the aerobatic wheelings of starlings. Expect some ups and downs and be prepared for mud after wet weather.

Map: OS Explorer OL20, South Devon, Brixham to Newton Ferrers 1:25 000

Start point: From the car parking area on the edge of South Hallsands with honesty box. Grid ref: SX816384. Nearby postcode: TQ7 2EY

Directions to start: Hallsands is on the coast, south of the A379 in South Devon

Parking: Car park as per start point above

Public Transport: No bus service to Hallsands. Nearest railway station is Totnes

Refreshments: None en route

Toilets: None en route

Nearby places to stay: Down Farm B&B, Start Point, 01548 511234

Nearby places of interest: Start Point Lighthouse, 01803 771802

Possible birds include: Blackbird, blue tit, carrion crow, chaffinch, fulmar, gulls, pheasant, robin, shag, skylark, starling, stonechat, woodpigeon, wren, yellowhammer

Authors' tip: Carry refreshments with you and check visiting times for Start Point Lighthouse perhaps allowing time for a tour during the course of your walk

Leave the car park and turn right down the lane. You quickly pass the complex of Prospect House with its various mews apartments on your left. The lane climbs and as it starts to go left downhill look for the access on the right to the ruined village viewing platform. Go down here to see what's left of the old Hallsands – there is a collection of information boards explaining the history of the homes that were destroyed in the wake of commercial enterprise further along the coast.

Climb back up the slope towards Prospect House and as you rise back up to the lane look left to where a two-way fingerpost indicates the coast

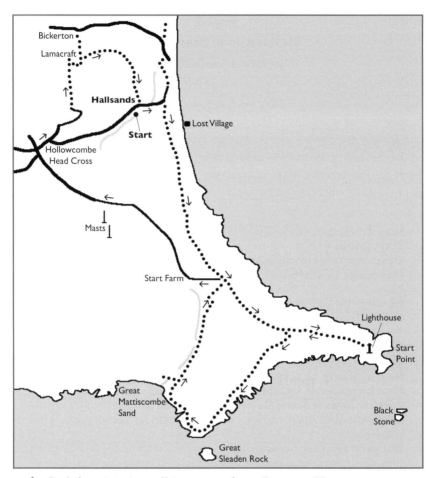

path. Go left to join it, walking away from Prospect House, sea to your left towards Start Point and its lighthouse, 1¼ miles away.

The path becomes more open, enjoying good coastal views in both directions. Don't forget to look behind, across the Dart Estuary towards Froward Point; if conditions are clear, you may make out the daymark tower poking up on top of the headland (see feature on Kingswear walk). Also in that direction lies the long expanse of Slapton Sands and, behind it, Slapton Ley, the largest, natural freshwater lake in south west England. The path leads unerringly into Start Point Car Park above the lighthouse. Pass through the large gates (or cross the adjacent stile) to a three-way fingerpost and from here head down the now-surfaced coast path towards Lannacombe. At the next three-way fingerpost you have an option; to see the lighthouse keep going downhill to Start Point (although you will shortly be returning to this post to continue with the coast path). The solid lighthouse commands a wonderfully isolated spot. It is administered by Trinity House, an historic charity that originates from a fraternity of seafarers called The Guild of the Holy Trinity. This guild regulated the pilotage of shipping in waters used by Henry VIII and the charity received a Royal Charter in 1514. Nowadays Trinity House is best known for its administration of the lighthouse system of England, Wales, the Channel Islands and Gibraltar but also provides other aids to navigation such as lightships, buoys and satellite navigation. It also licences and supplies deep sea pilots who assist ships with navigation. Another less familiar aspect of its work is the provision of retirement homes for ex-mariners.

Return back up the path to the fingerpost and turn left, leaving the surfaced path and striking out across the cliff towards Minehead, 462 miles away in Somerset at the end (or start) of the South West Coast Path. You swiftly crest the 'spine' along the headland, at which point a superb panorama awaits. Savour it, then continue on the yellow-arrowed, acorn-waymarked coast path, sea to your left – a fabulous stretch of walking across an area known as 'The Benches'; the path is clear and occasionally rocky. Keep going until you round the headland, the view across

Start Point and its lighthouse

Hallsands Lost Village

Details of the earliest settlement at Hallsands are shrouded in the mists of history but a chapel existed here in the early 16thC. In the 18th–19th centuries the fishing village expanded until it comprised almost 40 houses, including an inn with stables and a shop; the 1891 census tells us that there were  159 inhabitants most of whom owned their property having bought it when the previous owner of the estate died in 1857. However at the end of the 19thC Devonport Dockyard near Plymouth was expanded, a project requiring a huge quantity of raw materials such as sand and gravel. Dredging for these was carried out near Hallsands. The villagers were concerned for the safety of their homes as the beach began to drop away, leaving the village more exposed to high tides. They voiced their objections but dredging was permitted to continue until 1902. Once it ceased the level of the beach started to recover but the village's defence against violent seas was impaired and subsequent storms over successive winters caused much damage. By 1917 Hallsands' defences were breached leaving only two of the higher houses undamaged. The final resident was a Mrs Elizabeth Prettejohn who lived there until her death, aged 80, in 1964.

Lannacombe Bay opens up ahead with Prawle Point, the most southerly part of Devon, jutting into the sea beyond.

Once the view across the bay is revealed keep following occasional coast path posts. After about 200m you will reach one with a yellow hat whose badge indicates Pear Tree Cove (grid ref SX819367). From here look ahead to where the path forks in 100m, beyond the fork is a bench. The right-hand fork is your onwards route but first relish the bench with its view over Great Mattiscombe Sand; note its dedication to John Barlee, a naturalist and ornithologist "who loved this place". We met a couple here whose dog once went over the cliffs nearby – 14 coastguards rescued him and he lived to tell the tale.

A path near the bench leads down to the beach but the walk heads inland to a three-way fingerpost in a short distance, where the coast path continues to the left. Here you leave the coast path and continue inland towards the car park at Start Point. Pass through a gate in about 50m then continue along the side of a pretty coastal valley, the path is well-trodden.

After almost ½ mile you arrive back near the car park; go through the gate/over the stile then leave the car park along the lane, passing the entrance to Start Farm and its nearby twin masts. There are excellent inland views along this stretch of lane walking, shadows chase across the landscape and far in the distance you can see Dartmoor. The lane passes ivy-clad ruins on the right about ½ mile from Start Farm, and about 200m further on you reach the junction of Hollowcombe Head Cross. Turn right towards South Hallsands and in 100m the lane forks. If you wish to take a shortcut back to the car follow the lane to the right, otherwise go left towards Lamacraft Farm. The lane leads down to Lamacraft House and The Priory, the latter serving as a retreat. Look out for the lovely stone horse trough on the left with a pennywort-clad wall behind it. The arched gate to Lamacraft House is in front of you and the lane bends sharp right. Keep following it and it soon swings right again to pass behind The Priory, at which point don't go right but look for the small gap in the wall straight ahead.

Go through this gap on to a trodden earth and stone path, heading downhill away from the buildings between trees. This path descends for

Great Mattiscombe Sand

The coastline towards Hallsands

about ¼ mile before depositing you in the environs of some rather lovely houses near a two-way fingerpost. Take the right-hand option, heading uphill on a broad track, passing the sign for Orchard House. The track leads through a gate into a field. Pass through the field, boundary and sea views to your left. The boundary descends to reach a stile, beyond which you'll find the lane and car park from which you started.

The hamlet of Bickerton

Walk 6
Salcombe Estuary & Bolt Head
Distance: 4¾ miles / 7.6km

The South Hams is rich with boat-studded estuaries and river views, and is renowned for its glorious coastline. The Salcombe Estuary, encountered on this walk, is, in fact, a ria or 'drowned' valley rather than a true estuary. No significant river runs into it and it was created by rising sea levels flooding a valley, which also gave rise to all the little inlets surrounding the ria. This beautiful, view-filled route has the enticement of a well-appointed 'walkers' hut' at East Soar Farm, a delightful place of sustenance and shelter. The going can be rough underfoot and there are a few ups and downs.

Map: OS Explorer OL20, South Devon, Brixham to Newton Ferrers 1:25 000

Start point: Car park near Bolt Head Air Field. Grid ref: SX712375. Nearest postcode is TQ7 3DR which is 0.6 of a mile beyond the car park

Directions to start: The start point can be accessed off the A381 along lanes for 2 miles, south of the village of Malborough

Parking: Car park near Bolt Head Air Field

Public Transport: Malborough, the nearest village 2 miles away, is served by bus operators Tally Ho! and Stagecoach. Timetables available online at www.travelinesw.com. Nearest railway station is Ivybridge

Refreshments: The Walkers' Hut, East Soar Farm; 01548 561904

Toilets: Facilities at East Soar Farm – please make a donation

Nearby places to stay: The Bolthole, Malborough, 01548 561388

Nearby places of interest: Overbeck's (NT), Sharpitor, Salcombe: 01548 842893

Possible birds include: Blackbird, blue tit, buzzard, carrion crown, cormorant, goldfinch, gulls, house sparrow, kestrel, linnet, magpie, meadow pipit, peregrine, raven, shag, skylark, stonechat, swallow, wheatear, whitethroat, willow warbler, woodpigeon, wren, yellowhammer

Authors' tip: For a guided tour with a difference you can visit the nuclear bunker at the airfield, by prior arrangement – e-mail salcombebunker@gmail.com or call 07970 251386

Near the entrance to the car park is an information board about the RAF and Bolt Head. A fingerpost stands nearby; follow the finger towards Salcombe, Overbecks and Sharp Tor, passing through a gate and along the broad track. To your left are the buildings and hardware associated with the airfield. Follow the track as it bends about, ignoring any paths

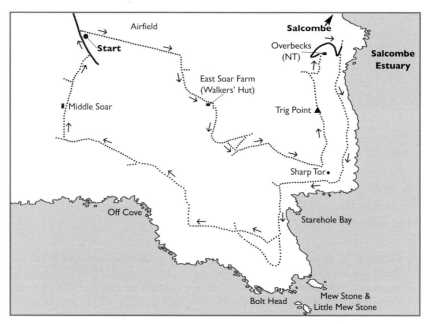

Airfield

Start

Salcombe

Overbecks
(NT)

**Salcombe
Estuary**

East Soar Farm
(Walkers' Hut)

Middle Soar

Trig Point ▲

Sharp Tor •

Off Cove

Starehole Bay

Bolt Head

Mew Stone &
Little Mew Stone

off, until you reach the buildings of East Soar Farm in just over ½ mile.
Check out the hut!

Beyond the barns go through a kissing gate and bear right across the field
in the direction of the arrow, to a gate you can see in the boundary. Once
through this follow the line of the right-hand boundary down the field

Walkers' Hut at East Soar Farm

to the bottom corner, where the path narrows between gorse, still going downhill. You arrive at a fence in front with the corrugated roof of a large barn visible in the valley beyond and a gate to your right. At the time of writing the three-way fingerpost was reclining on its back, fingers akimbo. From here go left, away from the gate, towards Sharp Tor, Overbecks and South Sands, walking uphill between gorse and following the line of the fence on the right. Within 100m you arrive at another three-way fingerpost. Here go obliquely right, still in the direction for Sharp Tor, Overbecks and South Sands, heading across the field towards a gate.

Go through the gate and across a small stone bridge to reach a two-way fingerpost. Go left at the post, uphill on a broad path, and keep ahead on

The Salcombe Estuary from Sharp Tor

this track, enjoying occasional views down to the right into Starehole Bay and keeping an eye open for attractive Herdwick sheep who graze the area. Keep following this lofty path above the coast until you land at a bench by a superb viewpoint with a 'direction indicator'. This is Sharp Tor. From here you can look left along the estuary, the town of Salcombe on its left bank and the golden beaches of East Portlemouth on its right-hand side. Along the coast ahead you can see to Prawle Point, the most southerly tip of Devon.

From here continue on the path as it now heads up the estuary, through an occasional gate and passing a trig point to the left of the path about

Bolt Head Airfield

The RAF presence in the Bolt Head area dates back to World War II. The grass airfield was constructed after the harvest in 1940 when hedges were removed and the area converted from agricultural use. It was operational from 1941 until 1945 and had two runways consisting of coconut matting overlaid with metal grids. It served as a busy satellite airfield to RAF Exeter. In later years a nuclear bunker was constructed here which was in use during the Cold War. The airfield now has just a single runway, which is differently aligned to the war time runways, and is used for private light aircraft. A usually peaceful area, it's hard to imagine how it once thrummed with Spitfires and Typhoons. The airfield is now operated by Bolt Head Aero Club and has hosted air displays in recent years which have seen return visits from wartime planes such as Hurricanes and Spitfires.

350m from the viewpoint. The path reaches descending steps at the bottom of which you find a three-way fingerpost. Turn right towards Overbecks and Salcombe, walking beneath trees as the path winds down. Soon you'll be walking beside the stone boundary wall of Overbecks with its lush, tropical vegetation; you'll see the house over the wall. At the lane turn left away from the entrance, enjoying the furry trees and descending very steadily as the lane bends about, you may glimpse South Sands below to the left if the trees aren't too leafy.

Palm trees at Overbecks

About 350m from the entrance to Overbecks you reach a three-way fingerpost at a sharp right turn and here you join the acorn-waymarked coast path signed for Starehole, ¾ mile away. The way is obvious now as the path starts to climb, sea to your left. You soon pass Bar Lodge on the left and a National Trust sign denoting the area of Bolt Head; keep going on the broad, stony track. You will pass occasional gates and rocky steps, the surroundings becoming increasingly craggy and dramatic until, over 600m from Bar Lodge you will be beneath the viewpoint at Sharp Tor, where you stood earlier. Here there are railings to prevent you from becoming part of the panorama. As you continue round the headland the view opens across Starehole Bay; eventually the path broadens and gates

Starehole Bay and Sharp Tor

lead across a small stone bridge to a three-way fingerpost denoting the area of Starehole. To your right now is the delightfully-named valley of Starehole Bottom but your way continues ahead on the coast path, sea to your left, towards Bolt Head, Soar Mill Cove and Bolberry.

At the top of Bolt Head you find a bench to the memory of William and Marion Ferrier-Pryor affording good views down to the gull-drenched Mew Stones just offshore. Keep going uphill beyond this to a three-way fingerpost by a gate whose badge denotes Bolt Head. Keep on the coast path towards Soar Mill Cove, to your right you can see the buildings of East Soar Farm and the airfield beyond; there are good views in all directions from this clifftop path and you may see ponies grazing, an aid to keeping the habitat in order.

View from Bolt Head

You reach another kissing gate about 40m to the left of a three-way fingerpost (its badge shows grid ref SX718367). Keep ahead on the coast path towards a yellow-arrowed post at SX717367. Then continue to the fingerpost by a gate you can see in the wall opposite, about 100m away. Here the three-way fingerpost shows grid ref SX716367 and you leave the coast path at this point on the inland path towards Middle Soar and Soar Mill Cove, following the wall on your right. You reach a four-way fingerpost by a gate. Go right, through the gate towards Malborough, walking through the field with the boundary to your left. Soon you pass Middle Soar Farm, keep going along the track passing an arrowed post in the field and staying with the curvy track until you reach the gate leaving Middle Soar. Turn left along the lane and in just over 100m you will be back at your start point.

Walk 7
East Prawle & Prawle Point
Distance: 4 miles / 6.4km

A walk of wonderful, panoramic views, dramatic coastal scenery and lovely coves. The National Coastwatch Institute Station at Prawle Point makes for an interesting visit; when volunteers are on duty they are happy to chat about their work and it's an opportunity to stock up on bottled water and pens! An excellent walk for birdwatching – you may see the rare cirl bunting – and many years ago one of the authors spotted an adder on the coast near here. Expect some bouldery bits along the coast and a steep uphill section near the end.

Map: OS Explorer OL20, South Devon, Brixham to Newton Ferrers 1:25 000

Start point: Near the shelter on the village green, almost opposite the toilets. Grid ref: SX780363. Nearby postcode: TQ7 2BY

Directions to start: East Prawle is situated near to the most southerly tip of Devon, south of the A379

Parking: Around village green, with an honesty box

Public Transport: A very limited bus service, details from www.coleridgebus.co.uk. Nearest railway stations are Ivybridge and Totnes

Refreshments: Piglet Stores and Café, East Prawle, 01548 511486; The Pig's Nose, East Prawle, 01548 511209

Toilets: At East Prawle, by village green

Nearby places to stay: Down Farm, Start Point, 01548 511234; West Prawle House, 01548 511277

Nearby places of interest: Visitor Centre at Prawle Point

Possible birds include: Blackbird, blue tit, buzzard, carrion crow, cirl bunting, great tit, gulls, jackdaw, kingfisher, little egret, long-tailed tit, moorhen, stonechat, woodpigeon

Authors' tip: Check out the website of the rather unique Pig's Nose Inn and try to time your visit for when this 'real ale' pub is open: www.pigsnoseinn.co.uk

---

Walk along the lane away from the toilets and the village centre, village green on your left. This is a signed public byway to Prawle Point. Follow the lane for 400m, then, when it bends sharp left, near a three-way fingerpost with the entrance to a house called Ash Park on the right, keep straight ahead on the public bridleway from which you will have sea views to your left as you proceed. Follow this clear track for about ¾ mile until it opens up at a T-junction of paths where there's a good view of Bolt Head across the bay, with the closer promontory of Pig's Nose jutting out

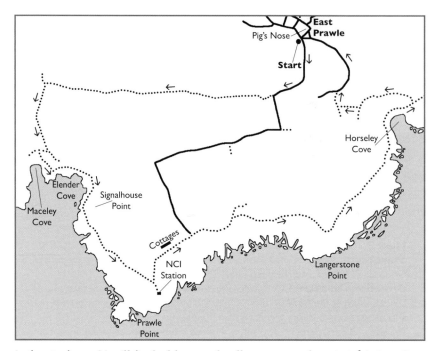

in front of you. You'll find a blue- and yellow-arrowed post at this junction; go left, following the yellow arrow of the footpath and leaving the blue bridleway. You're now following a narrower path between hedges.

The path descends and at its lower reaches becomes more open. You'll meet a post with lots of yellow arrows about 400m from the T-junction where you joined the footpath above. At this go sharp right, still downhill, zigzagging down to meet the acorn-waymarked coast path above Maceley Cove, as shown on the next post. Here go left, still heading seawards and now following the coast path, unless you wish to explore the path going right down into the attractive, sheltered Cove.

The coast path here is a glorious stretch of walking, make sure the sea is to your right. Some rock scrambling brings you on to the path above the more dramatic Elender Cove. Keep going, watching your step. Eventually you'll pass under the craggy bits of Signalhouse Point (shown on OS map), glance up at the cliff face above you where there's a memorial plaque to Judy Moore, in whose memory this area was given. The signalhouse, which was located on the cliffs nearby, formed part of a

The inviting beach at Maceley Cove

chain used to warn of possible invasion during the Napoleonic Wars. The plaque is easily missed, but the waymarked coast path is clear. Some way further on the NCI Station at Prawle Point appears; this is your next port of call and is approached by broad grassy paths leading across the headland. If the light is right you'll be treated to a glittering sun-path across the sea.

Beyond the NCI Station follow the clear coast path, passing a row of superbly-situated cottages on your left. Beyond them, ignore the

Elender Cove

East Prawle

Evidence of human occupation in this area dates back to several thousand years BC and the village gets a more 'recent' mention in the 11thC Domesday Book. East Prawle derives its name from the Anglo Saxon word 'Præwhyll' meaning 'lookout,' an undeniable asset of Prawle Point, the most southerly tip of Devon and a good vantage point from which to watch for potential invaders or struggling seafarers. The coast here is the site of many shipwrecks and smuggled booty from these was stored at the 500 year old village inn, The Pig's Nose. This remains popular today and has hosted such music legends as the Boomtown Rats, The Yardbirds and The Animals; the inn even boasts a dog menu!

fingerpost pointing left along a bridleway, and instead go through a gate to a three-way fingerpost on the far side, at grid ref SX775354 as shown on its badge. From here continue on the coast path towards Lannacombe. The way now is less rocky, a gentler part of the walk. About 300m beyond the cottages you meet another leftwards footpath near Langerstone Point (grid ref SX778355). Ignore this too, and stay on the coast path for almost another mile, glancing back from time to time to see the rock formation at the end of Prawle Point, a miniature version of Dorset's Durdle Door. Houses on the outskirts of East Prawle will eventually appear above you as you continue, they command excellent views.

Prawle Point and NCI Station

The coastline east of Prawle Point

After an enjoyable mile of walking from that ignored left path you reach a three-way fingerpost with a badge denoting Horseley Cove (spellings vary) at grid ref SX786360. Here you leave the coast path and follow the direction of the finger pointing inland along the bridleway to East Prawle, ½ mile away, which climbs gently between hedges. 300m from joining the bridleway it emerges from trees to reach an arrowed post. Here follow the yellow arrow, going right up stone steps to enter a field. Climb steeply, straight up through the field to the top boundary. At the top go right for a few metres to find a stone-stepped stile taking you over the pennywort-clad wall. Once over it turn right along the bridleway and soon you reach a rough-surfaced track between houses. Continue uphill, away from the houses on a tarmac lane, passing a house called Sea View on your right. This leads back to the centre of the village and The Pig's Nose.

East Portlemouth
Distance: 4¼ miles / 6.8km

This area is one of our favourite haunts; a glorious place for blue-sky days, when little coves, inlets and some of the county's most beautiful beaches will tempt you. Dog-friendly all year round, these beaches are an extremely beautiful part of the coastline. There's a good chance of seeing seals. The ambience of this area is steeped in the essence of 'al fresco'; soak it up. Apart from the long flight of steps from the car park, this is fairly easy walking though can be rough underfoot in places along the coastal stretch with a few ascents. Sheep graze the precipitous cliffs so if you have a dog with you don't let him send them over the edge!

Map: OS Explorer OL20, South Devon, Brixham to Newton Ferrers 1:25 000

Start point: East Portlemouth. Grid ref: SX746386. Postcode: TQ8 8PE

Directions to start: East Portlemouth is on the east side of the Salcombe estuary, south of Kingsbridge and can be accessed off the A379

Parking: There is an 'honesty box' area set aside for parking at East Portlemouth, high above the estuary overlooking the spectacular view. If this area is full there is an alternative National Trust car park at Mill Bay (SX741381) which is more expensive and shortens the walk

Public Transport: Buses run to Salcombe, from where the ferry runs to East Portlemouth. Details from www.travelinesw.com. Nearest railway station is Totnes

Refreshments: The Gara Rock, East Portlemouth, 01548 844810; Venus Café, East Portlemouth by the ferry, 01548 843558. If you take the boat across the estuary there are many places to eat around Salcombe

Toilets: By Venus Café and at Mill Bay Car Park

Nearby places to stay: West Prawle House, nr East Portlemouth, 01548 511277; Salcombe Harbour Hotel, Salcombe, 01548 844444; Tides Reach Hotel, South Sands, Salcombe, 01548 843466. There are numerous B&Bs on both sides of the estuary

Nearby places of interest: The National Trust's Overbecks, 01548 842893

Possible birds include: Chiffchaff, cirl bunting, cormorant, gannet, goldfinch, grey wagtail, gulls, kestrel, magpie, oystercatcher, robin, skylark, swallow, woodpigeon, wren, yellowhammer

Authors' tip: If time allows take the ferry over to Salcombe, it's a lovely way to approach this colourful and vibrant town

Emerge from your car, select a bench and absorb the views over the estuary. If you don't get any further today this alone is worth the trip. The car park leads to a grassy slope and thence to a gate with a narrow

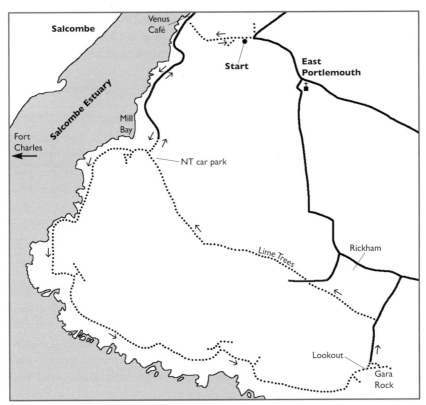

tarmac footpath beyond. A three-way fingerpost directs you down here towards the Passageway and Salcombe. Descend the steps and turn right for your first stop at the Venus Café, a wonderful spot at which to enjoy refreshments with a backdrop of Salcombe across the water and a hive of boating activity in the foreground.

Emerge from the Venus Café and turn right along the lane, passing the access to the ferry on your right. This can be a treat for later, time permitting. Follow the lane past lovely houses as far as Mill Bay which is the alternative parking/starting place. Find the three-way fingerpost that directs you right for Gara Rock, 2½ miles away, on the acorn-waymarked coast path and follow this into woodland.

When the path forks keep right ignoring the top path for Gara Rock. Enjoy tempting glimpses through the trees of golden sands and turquoise waters. When the path forks again your route climbs left through the trees, but we would recommend a short detour along the right hand path to admire an enticing beach; a fine stop for a picnic and a paddle. Return to the coast path and continue. Across the estuary you will see the beaches of South Sands to the left and North Sands to the right. Look out for the ruins of Fort Charles (see feature).

Keep on the well-trodden coast path as it winds under trees, estuary down to your right. Eventually the trees reduce and the views open up. The path comes round to a meeting of ways with a yellow-arrowed post and grid ref badge showing Rickham Common (SX736376). From here continue on the acorn-waymarked coast path, which is the most right of the options, nearest the sea. You have good views of the impressive headlands of Sharp Tor and Bolt Head across the water, which can be explored on the Salcombe Estuary walk.

The path curves to the left away from the estuary and along the coast with its richly coloured rock formations. Keep your eyes open for seals and, if you're lucky, a dolphin swimming by. Follow the coast path as it continues above Leek Cove and into the area of Gara Rock. Eventually the path ascends to a meeting of ways (SX750370). Don't take the top path to Mill Bay but continue on the coast path towards the little white, thatched lookout building that you'll see up on the cliff above. (*Before you reach this there is a right fork – coast path – leading to the attractive beach of Rickham Sands*

Wonderful view of Salcombe from East Portlemouth

East Portlemouth

In Mediæval times the area was a hive of industry, shipbuilding being an important source of revenue. During the 100 Years War with France 4 ships were sent from here to Crécy and Calais and over 200 years later another local vessel was involved in the defence against the Spanish Armada. In the  latter half of the 19thC the Duke and Duchess of Cleveland owned the estate and village. Big landowners of that era wielded huge power over tenants and the Clevelands decided to evict almost half the villagers from their cottages which were subsequently demolished. The land was turned over to three large farms for the benefit of the landowners. This inhumane act caused an outcry. The Duchess subsequently helped fund the restoration of the Parish Church of St. Winwaloe – whose spelling has varied over the centuries until in 2006 it reverted to the historically correct version.

Fort Charles (Salcombe Castle) was built in the reign of Henry VIII to defend the estuary against pirates. It became a busy place during the Civil War when Edmund Fortescue rebuilt it as a royalist stronghold in 1643. He named it Fort Charles in honour of the king. It was under siege from January to May 1646 and was the last place in the war to surrender to the Parliamentarians. It was then deliberately ruined by order of Parliament.

if you wish to explore, after which retrace your steps and join the distinct path up towards the Gara Rock complex and the white lookout.) Once used to keep an eye on smuggling, the lookout has wonderful views. A nearby information board tells you about the wrecks offshore. Partake of sustenance in the superbly situated Gara Rock Rotunda; rebuilt in 2013 on the site of an earlier hotel, which in turn had evolved from coastguard cottages. This venue is very walker-and-dog-friendly.

From Gara Rock proceed along a narrow lane in a northerly direction away from the coast, passing their car park. In 200m take the footpath on your left towards Mill Bay. This crosses a parking area then becomes a fenced path between fields, look way ahead to the distinctive shape of Malborough Church. The path goes under trees and reaches a meeting of ways. Descend steps and cross to a gate with a blue bridleway sign, continuing through this gate on the bridleway.

Rickham Sands as seen from Gara Rock

For dendrologists amongst you a real treat awaits. Ancient giants of pollarded lime trees accompany you for a while as you return towards Mill Bay. They are a remarkable sight. Beyond them the track continues back to Mill Bay Car Park where you now have two choices. You can either retrace your steps along the lane towards the Venus Café or, if tide permits, it's a pleasant diversion to make your way back along the sandy beaches as far as the ferry pontoon where you can ascend the steps back to the lane. If you take this latter option be aware, depending on the level of the tide, you may have some rock scrambling to do. Once back on the lane you are faced with the final climb up the steps to the top car park.

Pollarded lime trees

Walk 9
Harberton
Distance: 4¼ miles / 6.8km

A very pretty village with a characterful 13thC inn is the starting point of this walk. The inn, a former church house, is reputedly haunted by Mick the Monk, who has been known to appear in photographs. Nearby you may, if you're lucky, be able to top-up on marmalade, fudge, cakes and greetings cards at a sweet little wayside stall set into a garden wall. The route follows paths, tracks and occasional quiet lanes. Some areas can be wet underfoot. The ascents are not too dreadful, though sometimes lengthy, and the views are very good.

Map: OS Explorer OL20, South Devon, Brixham to Newton Ferrers 1:25 000

Start point: From outside the Church House Inn. Grid ref: SX777586. Postcode: TQ9 7SF

Directions to start: Harberton is 3 miles SW of Totnes and be accessed via lanes from the A385

Parking: With courtesy on the road in village

Public Transport: Harberton is served by the following bus operators: Tally Ho! and Harbourne Shuttle. Timetables available online at www.travelinesw.com. Nearest railway station is Totnes

Refreshments: Church House Inn, Harberton, 01803 863707

Toilets: None en route

Nearby places to stay: Church Barn B&B, Harberton, 01803 868652; Foales Leigh Farm B&B, Harberton, 01803 862365; Preston Farm B&B, Harberton, 01803 862235

Nearby places of interest: Totnes Castle, Totnes, 01803 864406; Totnes Elizabethan House Museum, Totnes, 01803 863821

Possible birds include: Buzzard, carrion crow, house martin, house sparrow, jackdaw, jay, rook, swallow, woodpigeon, wren

Authors' tip: If in the area for an extended period consider a trip along the River Dart from Totnes to Dartmouth. The Dartmouth Steam Railway and River Boat Company offer cruises along this most scenic of rivers (01803 555872)

Starting outside the Church House Inn, walk away from the church down the lane. Cross a small junction and keep straight on past St. Andrew's Cottages on your left. You reach the main lane through the village; turn right, passing the bus stop and phone box on your right, then keep ahead on the lane away from the centre of the village, passing lovely houses and a small junction called Triangle. The Harbourne River eventually joins

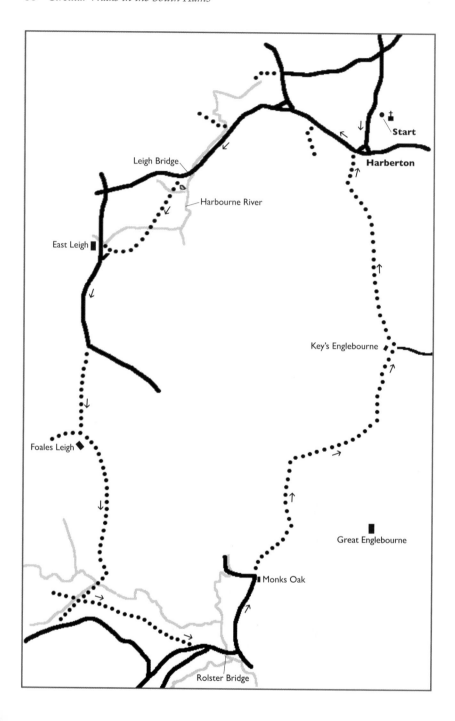

you, down on the right. The road crosses the river on a small stone bridge and you'll arrive at Leigh Bridge Cottage, where a footpath goes left off the lane. This is just over ½ mile from the centre of the village.

Here leave the lane and go left on the footpath, entering a field via a stile/gate and crossing the field in the direction shown by the yellow arrow. This line brings you to a gate into another field with an arrow on its post. Cross the field as directed, you are heading very slightly right up to the top boundary, crossing a damp area at the bottom of the field before you start to climb. When you reach the top boundary you'll find a gate on to a track. Pause here for a breather and to admire the view back towards Leigh Bridge Cottage and beyond.

Turn right along the track and follow it until it emerges on to a drive. Turn right, away from the house, and soon you'll reach the lane in the hamlet of East Leigh. Go left on the lane, enjoying expansive views. In about 400m the lane swings left at the entrance to Foales Leigh; here you'll see a footpath fingerpost pointing you straight ahead along their drive – follow this. In another 400m the drive swings left (straight on goes into a farmyard which you don't want). Go left with the drive, descending to cross a small ford (this may dry up) and passing the attractive buildings of Foales Leigh. The obvious track continues beyond, keep with it, rising gently before starting to descend, at which point you have glorious views to look forward to.

Track between Foales Leigh and Beenleigh Brook

Church houses were the mediæval equivalent of the village hall, their main purpose having been to raise funds for the church. Often they would be venues for church ales, a celebration consisting of sport, plays and morris dancing – all enhanced by a strong beer often brewed on the premises.

With the rise of Puritanism such festivities were deemed inappropriate and church houses were closed. After 1600 the buildings began to see use as schools, poor houses or inns as we see here in Harberton. Over 60 church houses are known to exist in Devon.

600m from Foales Leigh, as the track continues ahead into a field, look out for the yellow arrow which directs you left off the track, to enter an adjoining field beneath a hollow tree. Head down the field with the boundary to your right, aiming for a gap in the opposite boundary. Here another arrow directs you to continue downhill and you'll soon reach a

Harberton in sight

footbridge crossing the delightfully-named Beenleigh Brook. Beyond the bridge continue through the next field, boundary to your right, and in just over 100m you'll see a four-way fingerpost near another footbridge beneath the trees on the right. Turn left away from the post, still in the same field and now keeping the line of the top boundary to your right. At the end of the field you find a stile in the corner. Cross here and continue through the next field. The right-hand boundary soon ends, keep ahead, aiming for a bungalow across the field. To the right of this you'll find a gate leading on to the lane.

Turn left along the lane, ignoring a right turn in 100m and looking out for grazing alpacas. Cross Rolster Bridge, beyond which you soon reach a junction. Turn left and follow this lane for 400m to arrive at Monks Oak Farmhouse. Here the lane swings left but you keep ahead on the ascending green lane, probably the steepest part of the walk, but gradually the ascent lessens.

As you climb you'll pass gateways on your left, an opportunity to pause and enjoy views across East Leigh to the distant hills of Dartmoor. It can be tacky underfoot on this track. Keep winding up with it and eventually you'll be rewarded with a downhill stretch. After a left bend Harberton

St Andrew's Church, Harberton

will come into view ahead and soon you'll reach the farm of Key's Englebourne. Go left at the end of their lovely rounded wall, heading along another green lane. Beautifully dappled in sunny weather, this is another pleasant track but again can be wet underboot. The track continues for over 750m, eventually passing (avert your eyes) a tiny sewage plant down to the right then ascending to reach a T-junction of tracks. Go right here, heading downhill to arrive in the village at the bus stop. Bear right across the road to the junction then turn left to retrace your steps back up to the inn and the church.

Walk 10
Kingswear
Distance: 4¼ miles / 6.8km

An outstanding blend of fabulous coastline, majestic trees and layers of history are key ingredients of this walk. In summer the colours are lovely – we watched blue butterflies savouring yellow toadflax – and the cry of gulls will be with you all year round. Look out for peregrines, the fastest creature on earth, and listen for the chink of stonechats and the piping whistle of oystercatchers. Be prepared for a few steep ascents; the latter stretch of the walk can be very wet.

Map: OS Explorer OL20, South Devon, Brixham to Newton Ferrers 1:25 000
Start point: Brownstone Car Park near Coleton Fishacre. Grid ref: SX904509.
Nearest postcode: TQ6 0EQ
Directions to start: Brownstone Car Park is 2½ miles east of Kingswear and can be found along lanes from the B3205
Parking: Brownstone Car Park
Public Transport: Kingswear, the nearest village, is served by the Stagecoach bus operator. Timetables available online at www.travelinesw.com. Nearest railway station is Paignton
Refreshments: None en route but lovely Kingswear is a short drive away and offers a few places for refreshment. Coleton Fishacre (seasonal), 01803 752466
Toilets: None en route
Nearby places to stay: Kaywana Hall, Higher Contour Road, Kingswear, 01803 752200; Nonsuch House, Church Hill, Kingswear, 01803 752829
Nearby places of interest: The National Trust's Coleton Fishacre: 01803 752466; Dartmouth Castle (English Heritage): 01803 833588 or 839618
Possible birds include: Blackbird, buzzard, carrion crow, chaffinch, cormorant, dunnock, fulmar, great tit, gulls, house sparrow, jackdaw, kestrel, long-tailed tit, magpie, oystercatcher, peregrine, raven, robin, shag, siskin, spotted flycatcher, stonechat, swallow, willow warbler, woodpigeon, wren, yellowhammer
Authors' tip: Take your binoculars as there's a good chance of seeing seals basking on the rocks on and around the Mew Stone

---

From the car park turn right along the lane for about 150m until you find a three-way fingerpost. Take the footpath going right signed as a link to the coast path. This follows the edge of the field, farm house on your left, and emerges through a kissing gate on to a short path which joins a track. Follow the track away from the farm.

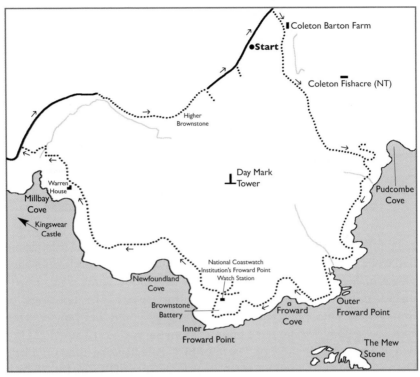

Keep ahead as you enter a field, still heading for the coast path – a lovely stretch of walking. At the end of this first field you enter a second, keep going with the boundary to your right. At the bottom of the field a two-way fingerpost directs you left still in the same field, continuing downhill with the boundary still to your right. You reach a stile with a lovely sea view, the huge Mew Stone is to your right along the coast. Continue beyond the stile to meet the coast path. Your way lies right towards Froward Point but first we recommend that you go left for a short way to admire the view into Pudcombe Cove from a convenient bench, and for a glimpse of the rather magnificent trees adorning the Coleton Fishacre Estate, just along the cliffs.

Once you've had enough follow the coast path south west for about 1½ miles towards Froward Point, sea to your left, enjoying the scenery, the birds and the seals. The lower rocks around the Mew Stone are often the favoured basking spot of the local seal colony; at the time of writing one of the regularly-seen adults was white.

Pudcombe Cove

Keep following the acorn-waymarked coast path beyond the Mew Stone and when the path forks keep left. As you round the headland you'll have views of Slapton Sands across the bay and Start Point away in the distance. Closer to hand you'll see the searchlight housings of Brownstone Battery before the coast path brings you right in amongst the ruins, a welcome shelter if it's raining. From the enclosed searchlight hut you have a good view of Dartmouth Castle (see feature on Little Dartmouth walk). Climb the steep steps to the gun platform, from which you can look down on the roofs of the searchlight huts, then beyond the platform walk up the line of the miniature railway which brought

The Mew Stone

Day Mark Tower and Brownstone Battery

This walk is notable for two man-made features: the Day Mark Tower and Brownstone Battery. The former is a listed building constructed in 1864. It is about 80 feet high and was built as a navigational aid for shipping, similar in purpose to a lighthouse but it has no light for night use – hence the name  'day mark'. A path from the car park leads past it.

Brownstone Battery was built in 1940 to protect the Dart Estuary against attack during WWII. Its extensive remains are a fascinating reminder of recent history and in one of the buildings up on the cliffs you will find the very modern-day station of the National Coastwatch Institute. Visitors are welcome to pop in to chat with the volunteers here and there is also an information centre in an adjacent building.

ammunition down to the guns. A nearby information board tells you all about it.

The tracks lead you to the ammunition store and the path continues up beside it, away from the sea and up more steps, passing more battery buildings, to reach the National Coastwatch Institution's Froward Point Watch Station. If volunteers are on duty they welcome visitors and will tell you about their work. On a hot summer's day they very kindly refilled our water bottles. Look inland from the NCI station and you will see the top of the day mark tower and, just across the grass, a four-way fingerpost by an information board. From the fingerpost take the coast path to Kingswear, 2 miles away. This path leads away from Froward Point, below the parking area and beside another battery building to head under trees. This is a pretty, undulating way along which you'll find another well-placed bench overlooking the coves and coast below.

A gate leads you out of the National Trust land of Higher Brownstone. Keep going, passing beneath superb trees and enjoying the pine needle-softened path beneath them. Another viewpoint (and first class picnic spot) affords a glimpse of Kingswear Castle on this side of the estuary beyond Mill Bay Cove. Across the water, above Dartmouth Castle, you can see a water tower at Jawbones.

Keep following the coast path until it descends steps to a two-way fingerpost by an unmissable turret in the grounds of a private house. Turn right along their drive and in about 20m, just before a cattle grid, go left to continue on the signed coast path. Pass through a gate and take a deep breath as a very uppish bit is ahead of you. Steps ascend through Warren Woods to eventually cross a welcomingly flat drive. Beyond this carry on up more steps until you reach another crossing drive beside a stone plinth bearing a plaque dedicated to the memory of Lt. Col. Herbert Jones, who preferred to be known as 'H'. He was killed in the Falklands and in 1984 this path through the woods was dedicated to his memory and opened to the public.

A nearby three-way fingerpost directs you right towards Brownstone, leaving the coast path to continue without you. Head along the surfaced track, refreshingly flat after the last bit and from which you still have coastal views. At a fork, in about 200m, keep right towards Brownstone, passing the elegant edifice of The Grange. Within another 200m, near Home Farm, a two-way fingerpost near a decorative telephone box directs you right, following a garden fence to your left. This stony path can be extremely wet as it climbs for nearly 400m to Crocker's Cottage. Continue along the drive beyond to arrive at Higher Brownstone Farmhouse where you'll see a three-way fingerpost beside the wall on the right. Keep ahead towards Coleton Fishacre, glancing right for another view of the day mark tower, keeping its eye on you across the fields. Follow the lane all the way back to the entrance to your car park.

Looking towards the castles

Walk 11
Little Dartmouth
Distance: 3¼ miles / 5.25km

This is an easy-to-follow gem of a route with stunning views, turquoise seas (light permitting) possible seals and the option to visit Dartmouth Castle if you wish to extend the walk. The cries of gulls and buzzards may mingle with the distant toot of steam trains, running between Paignton and Kingswear. There are a few ascents but only one is a bit of a puff and a bench will be waiting for you.

Map: OS Explorer OL20, South Devon, Brixham to Newton Ferrers 1:25 000

Start point: Little Dartmouth Car Park (National Trust). Grid ref: SX874491. Nearest postcode: TQ6 0JP

Directions to start: Little Dartmouth is south west of Dartmouth, off the B3205

Parking: Little Dartmouth Car Park (see above)

Public Transport: No buses to the start point although Dartmouth is well-served. The nearest train station is Paignton

Refreshments: Dartmouth Castle Tea Rooms, 01803 833897

Toilets: None en route unless you continue to Dartmouth Castle

Nearby places to stay: Greenswood Farm, Dartmouth, 01803 712100; Paper Moon, Dartmouth, 01803 833943

Nearby places of interest: Dartmouth Castle, Castle Rd, 01803 833588; Dartmouth Museum, Duke St, 01803 832923

Possible birds include: Blackbird, buzzard, carrion crow, chaffinch, cormorant, dunnock, fulmar, great tit, gulls, house sparrow, jackdaw, kestrel, long-tailed tit, magpie, oystercatcher, peregrine, raven, robin, shag, siskin, spotted flycatcher, stonechat, swallow, willow warbler, woodpigeon, wren, yellowhammer

Authors' tip: At Compass Cottage we recommend keeping ahead for a few metres before ducking right into trees to follow the South West Coast Path to Castle Point and Dartmouth Castle, about ¼ mile (0.4km) away. To resume the walk return to the fingerpost at Compass Cottage

---

Look for the three-way fingerpost in the car park and head along the public bridleway signed 'Diamond Jubilee Way'. This surfaced track passes some majestic trees and reaches the hamlet of Little Dartmouth where you'll see another three-way fingerpost. Keep straight on towards Dartmouth, 1¾ miles away, noting the dominant day mark tower on the headland beyond (see feature on Kingswear walk). Gateways afford

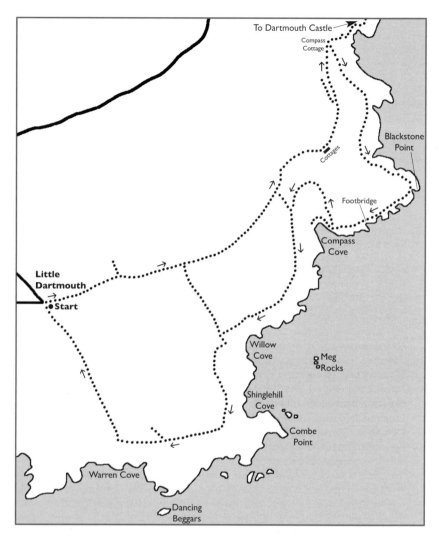

glorious views along the coast: behind you to Start Point with its lighthouse and the long, long stretch of Slapton Sands; in the other direction the mighty Mew Stone and, eventually, the mouth of the River Dart.

These initial views herald a superb panorama as the track emerges through a gate; if your timing and the weather is good sun-spangled water and yacht-studded estuary views await you. Keep ahead on the

Walkers with day mark tower in background

clear track, hedge to your left. Below you may spot a well-placed bench which you can perch on later. About ¾ mile from Little Dartmouth a gate brings you to the environs of a row of well-located cottages, pass them on your right and continue on the bridleway beyond.

As you proceed Kingswear Castle comes into view across the estuary and 400m from the row of cottages you reach a three-way fingerpost opposite Compass Cottage. Here you have a choice – the walk goes sharp right on the South West Coast Path back towards Little Dartmouth unless you are following the Authors' Tip, above. Continuing on the walk, after the

Shags spread their wings on Western Blackstone offshore

Dartmouth and Kingswear Castles

The mouth of the River Dart was always a potential weak spot in England's defences and during the Hundred Years' War with France (14thC–15thC) the town of Dartmouth suffered attacks. The need for defence was quite urgent and the two castles of Dartmouth and Kingswear were constructed.  A great chain was installed across the estuary which could be positioned at night to prevent the passage of ships. As gun range increased with improving technology weapons positioned at Dartmouth could fire further. This reduced the need for Kingswear's defensive role but Dartmouth Castle saw many battles and skirmishes and remained in active service right up to WWII. It is now cared for by English Heritage.

sharp right you immediately pass Wavenden on your left keeping ahead on the acorn-waymarked coast path, a lovely sylvan way with estuary views to your left through trees. The path descends and when it emerges from the trees you have clear views back towards Dartmouth Castle on this side of the estuary.

Enjoy this open coastal stretch and when you reach a fork keep left, descending three steps and skirting a dramatic rocky area to reach a footbridge in 300m. Glance up the inlet, then continue, ascending steps and soon arriving at a three-way fingerpost. Unless you wish to explore Compass Cove go right, over a stile and head inland. You soon join a well-trodden path (this was the right-hand option at the fork). Keep going and soon you climb to the bench which you saw earlier from above. Now you can make use of it. From the bench continue on the clear path as it bends its way back towards the coast.

You are still climbing gently to reach a wooden gate just over 100m from the bench. Keep straight on through this, ignoring the path arrowed right. At the next fork another yellow-arrowed post keeps you left along the coast path and about 600m from the gate you reach another inland option, but still you need to keep ahead on the coast path.

Sailing boats are plentiful on this section of coast

Beyond here we met a herd of beautiful White Park cattle, grazing the fields beside the path. Keep going, enjoying the views ahead. Eventually the church tower at Stoke Fleming appears and soon after that the coast path swings right, following a stone wall which becomes a fence. Little Dartmouth comes into view over to the right. Pass through a gate, following the broad path which brings you back into the car park from whence you started.

Grazing with a view!

Noss Mayo
Distance: 5 miles / 8km

Although the name is redolent of Southern Ireland, Noss Mayo is firmly in the South Hams and was named after 13thC landowner, Matthew, who was granted the local manor of Stoke by Edward ll. Early documentary evidence refers to the village as Nesse Matheu or Matthew's Nose. It probably started life as a fishing village, hence nearby Cellars Beach where fish were stored. This lovely walk takes in the beauty of South Devon's coastline, some idyllic creeks and an appealing village with excellent hostelries. The walking is relatively easy although there are steep bits to and from the beaches if you decide to visit them – which we would strongly recommend.

Map: OS Explorer OL20, South Devon, Brixham to Newton Ferrers 1:25 000

Start point: Noss Mayo. Grid ref: SX547474. Postcode: PL8 1EG

Directions to start: Noss Mayo is about 10 miles east of Plymouth, south of the A38

Parking: Car park in Noss Mayo next to tennis courts

Public Transport: Noss Mayo is served by regular, Tally Ho! buses from Plymouth. Timetables available online at www.travelinesw.com. Nearest railway station is Plymouth

Refreshments: The Ship Inn, Noss Mayo, 01752 872387; The Swan Inn, Noss Mayo, 01752 872392; Tea Gardens (seasonal) at No. 1 The Point, Noss Mayo, 01752 872210

Toilets: In parking area by creek inlet near village centre

Nearby places to stay: Broadmoor Farmhouse, 01752 880407; Revelstoke Coombe, Noss Mayo, 01752 872663; Worswell Barton Farmhouse B&B, Noss Mayo, 01752 872977

Nearby places of interest: Saltram (NT), Plympton, 01752 333503

Possible birds include: Blackbird, blue tit, buzzard, carrion crow, chaffinch, cormorant, little egret, goldfinch, green woodpecker, greenfinch, gulls, house martin, house sparrow, jackdaw, kestrel, long-tailed tit, magpie, mallard, oystercatcher, pied wagtail, raven, robin, shag, sparrowhawk, stonechat, swallow, treecreeper, wheatear, whitethroat, woodpigeon, wren

Authors' tip: After sampling the local brew (in moderation, of course) we suggest you allow yourself time and daylight to explore this lovely village with its attractive cottages

Leave the car park and turn left along the lane, passing a playground on the left followed by access into the Woodland Trust-owned Brooking's

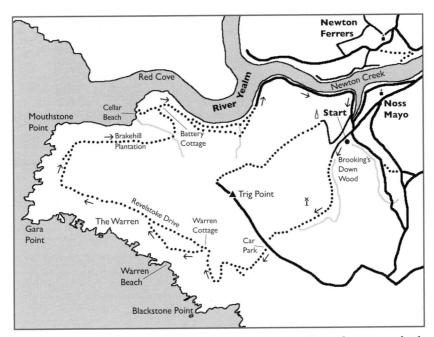

Down Wood. Don't enter the woods but continue along the lane, which soon becomes a track. Gradually you leave Noss Mayo behind you and reach a pair of semi-detached houses with barns on your right. Continue past them heading uphill along the track.

You reach a lane, turn left for 50m and then take the footpath on the right over a stile beside a car park serving the National Trust area of The Warren. Pause at the stile to look behind at the distant hills of Dartmoor, then continue on the path and through a gate, beyond which you go right on the broad track which, in just over 100m, is joined by the main coast path. The sea is down to your left with expansive views ahead across Wembury Bay, the Mew Stone loafing around offshore. (See feature on Wembury walk.)

The path here is unusually wide for the coast path and was constructed in the late 19thC to accommodate the carriage of the local landowner, Lord Revelstoke, enabling him and his guests to enjoy the scenery while his horses took the strain. Soon you approach Warren Cottage, built for posh Revelstoke picnics. Just before you reach it (grid ref: SX536465) take

View of coast near Warren Cottage

the left fork down off the 'Revelstoke Drive' and keep descending on a lovely, airy path until you reach an arrowed post with 'Warren Beach' etched on its far side (grid ref: SX533465).

From the post go left along the clifftop for 40m, where you will find steps leading down to Warren Beach; there are some comfortably flat rocks on which to picnic and nice rock pools. Then return back up to the post and take the narrow but obvious path going obliquely left uphill, hopping over a small crossing path, negotiating gorse bushes and continuing to climb steadily until you rejoin the broad coast path.

The hard rock café at Warren Beach

Eddystone Lighthouse

On a clear day, way out to sea off Plymouth, can be seen the 49m high Eddystone Lighthouse. The building which stands today is the fourth to be constructed. The first was completed in 1698, a wooden structure designed by Henry Winstanley. Five years later, in November 1703, its designer was in residence, undertaking some work on the structure, when a massive storm blew up. The lighthouse was wiped out and poor old Winstanley went with it; sadly his body was never found. Rudyerd's Lighthouse then followed and this was first lit in 1709. The third lighthouse to be built on the site is nowadays well-known to the people of Plymouth as its top section, known as Smeaton's tower, was re-erected on Plymouth Hoe. The current lighthouse was built by James Douglass. It was first lit in 1882, automated in 1982 and is now maintained by Trinity House, the General Lighthouse Authority, which itself was granted a charter in 1514 by Henry VIII (see main text in Hallsands Walk).

Turn left, sea down to your left, and keep going. This is superb walking; on a clear day you can see the Eddystone Lighthouse out to sea, 13 miles south west of Plymouth.

As you round the headland Wembury Church comes into view across the Yealm Estuary. Keep on the path above the water, enjoying the views – if you wish to explore the headland opposite you can do so on the Wembury walk. The path continues through Brakehill Plantation and eventually leaves the area of The Warren, continuing on a track past a row of white cottages before reaching the large and arresting Battery Cottage with its fascinating roof lines. At Battery Cottage look out for the footpath on the left, this will take you down to Cellar Beach should you wish to go there. Otherwise continue on the main track as it goes through Passage Wood. You will reach an information board on the left about this woodland.

Oystercatchers frequent the River Yealm

From here take the footpath going left off the track, an idyllic little path through the trees that eventually brings you to a kissing gate beside Ferryman's Cottage. Beyond here you reach the old Toll House with its display board of historic ferry fees. Should you slip into a time warp at this point it will cost you three old pennies (1p) to get your ass across the water. The whistles of the oystercatchers are free of charge.

Sampling an ale or two at The Ship Inn is a great way to finish

Beyond here continue on the drive away from the houses, eventually joining the lane along the banks of Yealm Pool and then Newton Creek, down to your left. Opposite a lay-by you'll see a path down to Kilpatrick Steps. Keep on the lane, unless you wish to explore, passing the seasonal ferry and enjoying the scenery of the creek. As you enter the village you will find a tempting, seasonal tea gardens at No. 1 The Point; they also sell attractive, driftwood craft. The lane continues to eventually pass The Ship Inn, which also calls loudly. Soon you see the village hall ahead. Here bear left with the lane to cross the head of the creek, then continue uphill back to the area of the village in which you should find your car.

Walk 13
Blackawton
Distance: 6 miles / 9.7km

Once you've torn yourself away from the historic gem of the church (see Authors' tip) the route is enticing, with expansive, undulating hill views and two good inns to refresh you on your return to the village. It can be very wet and sticky in places and there are some ups and downs, with one long ascent out of The Gara valley.

Map: OS Explorer OL20, South Devon, Brixham to Newton Ferrers 1:25 000

Start point: Outside the Parish Church of St. Michael. Grid ref: SX804509. Postcode: TQ9 7BE

Directions to start: Blackawton is 9½ miles south of Totnes and can be accessed of the A381/A3122

Parking: Park on road, please exercise courtesy towards residents

Public Transport: Limited bus service, details from www.travelinesw.com. The nearest train station is Totnes

Refreshments: The George Inn, Blackawton, 01803 712342; The Normandy Arms, Blackawton, 01803 712884

Toilets: None en route other than the inns

Nearby places to stay: The George Inn, Blackawton, 01803 712342; The Normandy Arms, Blackawton, 01803 712884

Nearby places of interest: Dartmouth Castle, Castle Rd, 01803 833588; Dartmouth Museum, Duke St, 01803 832923

Possible birds include: Blackbird, buzzard, carrion crow, dunnock, goldfinch, great tit, gulls, house sparrow, jackdaw, jay, magpie, mallard, pied wagtail, raven, robin, starling, woodpigeon

Authors' tip: Start your walk with a visit to the parish church of St. Michael, with its picturesque Jacob sheep who keep the graveyard in order, the view south towards Blackawton's arboreal 'sleeping giant' whom you can see reclining on the far hillside and, inside the church, the remarkable rood screen. This was commissioned to celebrate the wedding of Henry VIII to Katherine (sic) of Aragon – look for their initials in the panelling near the pulpit

Start from the main lychgate into the church near the stone Blackawton Village sign. Walk downhill along Main Street below the churchyard and in a very short distance you reach Cousins Cross. Turn right here up Park Lane, the churchyard still above you, and in about 50m take the next right towards the school. Just beyond the school, before an electricity sub-

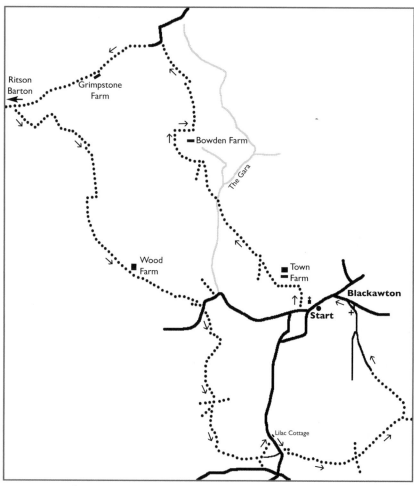

station and the entrance to Town Farm, you see a public bridleway going left off the lane.

Follow this, heading across the field towards a gate in the far boundary. In the next field head diagonally right down to the bottom corner where you find a gate with a three-way fingerpost beyond. Go right to another gate a few metres away and once through this a blue-arrowed post points you left. This leads damply down to another gate, go through and follow the direction of its arrow diagonally right across the field, down to a further gate. In the next field follow the right-hand boundary, dropping gently downhill, you may hear the babbling Gara in the valley down to your left. Another gate leads to an arrowed post directing you obliquely left down towards the bottom of the field. Here you find a wooden, and sometimes slippery, footbridge crossing The Gara. If the sun is out enjoy this lovely sylvan area of dappled light and sparkling water.

A metal gate beyond the bridge leads on to a clear track. Trudge breathily up this and eventually views open up to the right and behind you, taking

your mind off the ascent. The path swings left and a little over 300m from The Gara you reach a three-way fingerpost. Ignore the footpath left and keep ahead to a two-way fingerpost in a few metres. Here a gate leads into a field and you continue to the right on the bridleway, looking out for wild pansies and passing the left-hand end of the barns of Bowden Farm. Near the barns a fingerpost points you along a track round the end of the building to another post about 75m away. At this second post enter the field and glance leftish for a glimpse of distant Dartmoor, then turn right to follow the field's right-hand boundary. This brings you to a

Fan vaulting on rood screen at St. Michael's

fingerpost by a gate, go through and turn left along the surfaced track, away from the farm.

Follow this for almost ½ mile to where it emerges at the bend of another surfaced track. Now turn left and keep on the track as it drops to Grimpstone Farm in about 500m. When we last passed by there was a well- carved bear outside the farm, keeping a beady eye on us. Greet him if he's there then keep going beyond the outbuildings, rising and falling with the track as it becomes unsurfaced and potentially muddy. About 300m beyond the farm the track leads to a gate. Don't go through but

The Gara Valley

instead veer left to follow a narrower path downhill towards trees and a stream. Hop across the water and continue up the path beyond, climbing for about 150m until just before the buildings of Ritson Barton, you'll see a fingerpost on the left.

Follow its direction left through the field on a track which crosses a stream, then pass through an ancient tree-topped boundary about 120m from the fingerpost. Keep in the same direction beyond this – glance back to make sure you're still in line with the finger – and when you reach the

Farmland Views

footpath arrows on the boundary fence turn left, staying in the same field, approaching trees and the stream again. At the bottom of the field go right through the footpath gate and walk along the bottom of the next field – the stream is to your left under trees. You reach a stile and a short way beyond it an arrowed post tells you to bear slightly right to the far side of the field to a little wooden footbridge.

Cross this and a gate takes you into the next field. Follow the left boundary round the field, a well-rounded hillside up to your right, stream to the left and tussocks underfoot. At the far side follow the hedge round to a gate, go through and walk across the next field, stream still away to your left but further down the field now. At the far side a gate leads you into another field; the arrow here is misleading – walk across the top of the field following the boundary to your right. This leads to a gate on to a narrow, hedged path which soon opens out; continue ahead past a stone building on the right to reach a surfaced track. Turn left.

You approach the buildings of Wood Farm, a poetic place – look out for verses on the woodshed and elsewhere. In the yard an arrow directs you straight ahead, passing a house on your left to follow a tree-flanked path past outbuildings. You soon enter a field with a moss-and-navelwort-adorned stone wall on your right. Follow this boundary across the field then keep on through a further field to a footpath gate on the far side. Go through here and turn left down a narrow, fenced path, which turns right at the stream to follow it on your left. Keep going until the path swings right and brings you out to a surfaced drive. Turn left along the drive away from the house and descend to the lane. Turn right.

Follow the lane uphill for about 50m to a footpath sign on the left, which points you into an attractive collection of houses and barns. Walk across their yard and bear right in front of The Linney to a tall, wooden gate with a faded yellow arrow. Through here you'll find a clear path which takes you past a selection of buildings and brings you to a gate. It can be quite wet beyond here; you reach a footbridge with a gate beyond entering a field. Go right as directed, field sloping up to your left as you follow the bottom boundary. At the end of the field continue through the next and at the far side exit via a gate/stile on to a path. Ignore the stile to the left and go downhill for about 20m to a well-arrowed post. Here

Blackawton International Festival of Worm Charming
The idea of an annual worm charming festival was conceived in 1983, allegedly the result of an indulgent evening in one of the local inns. The first competition took place in 1984 and proved a popular event for many years until 2001, when the event was thwarted by various factors including the threat of Foot and Mouth Disease. It seemed that Blackawton's tradition of worm charming might die. Luckily a new Worm Master stepped in to resurrect the event, which goes from strength to strength. It's a vibrant day of music, ale, fancy dress, and all kinds of worm- and non-worm-related activities. Check the website for details of forthcoming charmings: www.wormcharming.co.uk. This is why Britain is Great!

veer right round the end of the hedge in front of you then walk ahead (more or less in the same direction as before), keeping the boundary to your left with an open meadow to your right and a stream over on the far side of it. You'll see a stile across to the right which you don't want, follow the left boundary for about 100m until the path ducks left through it, continuing in the same direction. Go through a gate and up stone, fern-fringed steps to follow the path under trees, passing an idyllically-situated garden and house to your right.

The path bends right and drops to meet the drive, go left away from the house. As the drive starts to gently ascend look for the fingerpost pointing you left, up to a gate. Go through here and up the field, following its right boundary up to the corner. Another yellow-arrowed gate takes you into a further field where you're heading towards the gable end of Lilac Cottage. You reach a 'combo' stile of wood, stone and metal, after which steps drop you on to the lane. Go right, downhill, for about 100m to a footpath on the left.

Follow this path, walking between a barn on the right and block wall on the left. Cross a small stream and bear right, passing an open-fronted shed on the left, then veering left to an arrowed gate – the arrow was rather obscured at the time of writing. Go through here, up a rough path and enter a field. Walk across the field past a telegraph pole with a helpful arrow. This is a lovely traverse with the meandering stream down to your right, though you may feel as if your left leg is shorter than your right by the time you get across – it would help if it were! At the far side look back to enjoy the view then cross the stile on to an enticing, tree-flanked path. Follow this to emerge at a crossing track by a two-way fingerpost. Cross the track and enter the field opposite, following its boundary on your right. This leads into a second field, the buildings of Pruston Barton over to your right. Veer slightly left of the track through the field to reach an arrowed stile in the far boundary with steps beyond. Descend to join a crossing bridleway and go left along it.

The sleeping giant

Keep on the track passing a house on your right in about 400m. The track becomes a lane on the outskirts of Blackawton; keep ahead as another lane comes in from the left in just over 300m. Pass a converted Wesleyan chapel, Ebenezer, on the left and its former Sunday School on the right. Notice the plaque on the latter and the names thereon, particularly one 'R.H. Bastard', a not unheard of surname in these parts. Keep ahead now along Chapel Street until you reach Normandy Cross at which point turn left to arrive back at your start point.

Ringmore & Kingston
Distance: 7½ miles / 12km

There are particularly lovely villages in this part of Devon and the two encountered on this walk are no exception. Add in beautiful beaches, fabulous coastal scenery, attractive woodland and a ruined mill – plus a very welcoming pub part-way round – and you have all the ingredients for a great walk. There are some strenuously steep sections interspersed with relatively easy bits, so be prepared for a puff. If you closely follow an OS map while walking you will notice a few variations from the printed path!

Map: OS Explorer OL20, South Devon, Brixham to Newton Ferrers 1:25 000

Start point: Ayrmer Cove Car Park, Ringmore. Grid ref: SX649456. Nearest postcode: TQ7 4HR

Directions to start: Ringmore is east of Plymouth and can be accessed off the A379

Parking: National Trust car park for Ayrmer Cove, clearly signed from centre of village

Public Transport: Very limited bus service, details from www.travelinesw.com The nearest train station is Ivybridge

Refreshments: The Dolphin Inn, Kingston, 01548 810314; Journey's End, Ringmore, 01548 810205

Toilets: None en route other than the inns

Nearby places to stay: Kimberley, Ringmore, 01548 811115; Windwood Farm, Ringmore, 01548 810615

Nearby places of interest: South Devon Chilli Farm, Loddiswell, 01548 810314

Possible birds include: Blackbird, blue tit, buzzard, carrion crow, chaffinch, chiffchaff, cirl bunting, curlew, goldfinch, great tit, gulls, house sparrow, jackdaw, kestrel, magpie, oystercatcher, pheasant, raven, robin, skylark, song thrush, stonechat, woodpigeon, wren, yellowhammer

Authors' tip: Wander round Ringmore – there are some gorgeous houses to admire – and allow yourself time to enjoy the beaches

Set off on the clear path which leads from the car park near the information board. In about 120m you reach a footpath gate, beyond here go left on the bridleway. This is Smuggler's Lane; flanked by hazel and home to dormice (which you are unlikely to see) it was also once a route used by smugglers bringing contraband up from the sea to hide it at the

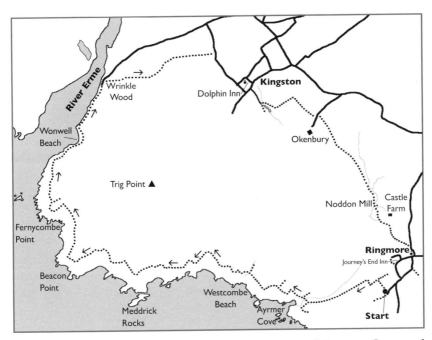

village inn. The path is heading for Toby's Point and Ayrmer Cove and descends towards the sea. Enticing views ahead soon open up and you arrive at the beach beside a large well-shouldered rock. This area is often alive with oystercatchers, their peeping whistle surrounding you as you walk. Turn right at the beach to join the coast path – there is an acorn

Ayrmer Cove

Towering cliffs are a feature on this section of coast

waymarker on a post near steps at the right-hand end of the beach. You are heading for Westcombe Beach; the sea is to your left. Pause occasionally as you climb to glance back at Burgh Island, just off the coast near Bigbury.

A knees-in-gear descent brings you to Westcombe Beach. From here you need the coast path towards Wonwell, ignoring the track inland to Kingston. A gate beyond the beach leads up to the cliffs and various paths head skywards – they merge at the top so follow whichever appeals most, but the closer to the edge you are (please be careful) the better the view

The Erme Estuary

Noddon Mill

The rather sad remains of this old corn mill
were consolidated by the National Trust in
2002 to prevent further deterioration. The
mill adjoined the cottage, and probably had an
'overshot' waterwheel powered by the flow
from a higher millpond. The Bigbury Census
of 1841 shows that James Taylor was miller
here with his wife, Joanna, and their three children, Catherine, Edward and
Jemima. The mill probably served Noddon Farm, situated about ½ mile to
the north east, as well as the village, which may have resulted in the access
track becoming a public path. A commercial directory of 1870 shows a
James Taylor as miller and basket maker at Noddon Mill.

will be down to Hoist Beach (so-called as seaweed was once hoisted up
here for use as a crop fertiliser). A waymarked post at the top is a welcome
stop for a breather before entering the land of Scobbiscombe Farm, a good
conservation area and home to the rare cirl bunting.

Keep following the coast path past a robust granite bench and onwards,
passing, successively, Beacon Point, Fernycombe Point and Muxham
Point. The path veers round to head inland up the Erme Estuary, with
beautiful views upriver and across to boathouses and old coastguard
cottages. You arrive at Wonwell Beach, just under 2 miles from the post
above Hoist Beach. Here, depending on the position of the tide, you can
either walk along the beach to the slipway at the far end, or make use of
the path behind the beach until you reach steps on the left which descend
to join the lane up from the slipway.

Once on the lane walk away from the beach until, within 100m, you find
a footpath pointing you right into the trees of Wrinkle Wood and towards
Kingston, 1¼ miles away. The path winds steeply through this lovely,
light woodland to reach a stile into a field. Follow the right-hand top
boundary of the field to a stile on the far side, then continue as before
through the next field, Torr Down Farm is visible in the valley to your
left. Follow the boundary round to the end of the field where a gate leads
on to a hedged path. You soon reach a stile with a yellow-topped two-

way fingerpost beyond. Follow the finger pointing obliquely right across the field. At the far side another fingerpost directs you along the boundary keeping it on your right. You have expansive views to the left towards the southern aspect of Dartmoor. Continue through the next field, boundary still to your right, until you reach the lane. Turn right, heading into Kingston.

In just over 300m you reach Wonwell Gate Cross. Turn left and follow the church wall as it bends right and leads you to the Dolphin Inn, one of the friendliest places we have encountered. Pandora Dog was supplied with biscuits.

Wonwell Beach

Beyond the Dolphin Inn you reach a T-junction. Turn right and in just over 50m, at Rock Cottage, go left. The lane descends between houses and becomes rough underfoot until, 150m from the turning, you find a two-way fingerpost under trees. Ahead is a bridleway, which you don't want, to the left is a footpath to Ringmore, 1½ miles away, which is the way you're going. Walk between the house and its garage (please respect their privacy) to join the footpath into the field (a yellow arrow directs). Follow the direction of the arrow to the right, keeping the fence to your left with ponds down to the right. You enter light woodland, the path winding through to reach steps up to a stile. Beyond this walk up the field, boundary to the left. Before entering the next field a post points you right, staying in the same field and still keeping the boundary to your

A warm welcome awaits at The Dolphin Inn in Kingston

left; a pleasant stretch of walking. A stile leads into the next field, continue along the left boundary until you reach the lane.

Turn left on the lane for a few metres, then go right on the signed footpath into a field, Ringmore is now 1¼ miles away. Go straight across to the far boundary where you emerge on to a track, turn left and follow the track as it immediately bends right. In 200m, at a fingerpost, go left off the track walking through the field with the hedge to your left. At the bottom swing right, still following the hedge until, in about 150m, the footpath goes left into Okenbury Plantation.

Follow the well-trodden path, invitingly downhill, through this lush woodland, a vast contrast to the mighty coastline of the earlier part of the walk. After a metal gate follow the arrowed path through a long, narrow field, there's a small, tree-flanked stream down to the left, woodland up to the right. Enter the next field where the path leads you to the ruined Noddon Mill. Here, go left to cross the stream, passing the ruins on your left and climbing the track ahead into the trees.

You reach a yellow-arrowed gate on the right, pass through and go up the next field as directed, bearing slightly left to a gate in the top fence. Go through it and turn left, following the line of the fence on your left with farm buildings below. Just before the corner of the field you find a kissing gate on the right. Go through and walk through the next field, boundary to your left; to your right a dip in the headlands gives a lovely seaward view. Within about 100m go through another kissing gate then follow the direction of the arrow diagonally across the field towards houses. There's a good view left to the turreted façade of Old Castle (formerly the rectory which was renovated during the mid 19thC in the Victorian Gothic style). In the far corner of the field a gate near a slate-hung house leads you into the next field. Walk diagonally across this as the arrow directs, heading towards another gate tucked under trees in the corner, adjacent to the garden wall of the attractive manor house.

You emerge on to the lane, turn right downhill to reach the junction outside the 13thC All Hallows Church, worth visiting to see the unusual mural and decorative rose window. From here the Journey's End Inn (if you wish to sample it) is down the lane to the right below the church, but the final stage of the walk follows the lane ahead, signed for the National Trust's Ayrmer Cove Car Park, just over 350m away. You will see the car park clearly signed off the lane at a left bend. An easy finish to a good walk.

Evening sunshine over Ayrmer Cove

Walk 15
Wembury & the River Yealm
Distance: 5¾ miles / 9.25km

Just a short distance from the hubbub of Plymouth, this walk is a great escape to the coast and countryside. With the mood of the sea and the landscape varying with the seasons, it's a rewarding route at any time of year. Starting with big sea views, the walk brings you into tranquil inland areas before landing you back on the beach. In summer you will see a wealth of butterflies; in autumn your picnic may be supplemented by blackberries. Watch out for the antics of surfers, listen for the 'yaffle' of green woodpeckers and, if you are an artist, take a sketch pad. You may encounter ponies grazing the Wembury cliffs as part of the habitat management. Expect some ascents and descents – it's worth the effort and there are many well-placed benches.

Map: OS Explorer OL20, South Devon, Brixham to Newton Ferrers 1:25 000
Start point: Wembury Beach Car Park (National Trust). Grid ref: SX518484. Postcode: PL9 0HP
Directions to start: Wembury is situated on the south coast of Devon, 6 miles south east of Plymouth. It can be accessed from the A379
Parking: Wembury Beach Car Park, as per start point above
Public Transport: Wembury is served by bus operators: First in Devon & Cornwall and Target Travel. Timetables available online at www.travelinesw.com. Nearest railway station is Plymouth
Refreshments: The Old Mill Café, Wembury Beach (seasonal), 01752 863280; The Odd Wheel, Wembury, 01752 863052
Toilets: At Wembury Beach
Nearby places to stay: Old Barton B&B, Wembury, 01752 863418; Worswell Barton Farmhouse, Noss Mayo, 01752 872977
Nearby places of interest: Wembury Marine Centre, Church Road, 01752 862538
Possible birds include: Blackbird, bullfinch, buzzard, carrion crow, green woodpecker, goldfinch, gulls, house martin, jackdaw, linnet, magpie, pied wagtail, raven, rook, swallow, swift, woodpigeon, yellowhammer
Authors' tip: After the walk why not relax a while at Wembury Beach and partake at the Old Mill Café

From the car park you have a clear view of the massive Mew Stone, just off the coast and watched over by the 15thC tower of St. Werburgh's

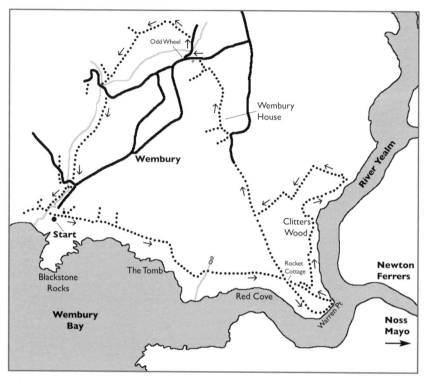

Church. Set out from the far end of the car park heading east with the sea to your right, this path is signed as a link to the coast path and rises to meet it – look out for the acorn waymark. Turn right along the coast path, away from Wembury Beach and the church. The path crosses the drive of some very well-positioned houses and continues, with views across the Yealm Estuary to Gara Point and out to sea. Ignore any turnings inland and keep going as the coast path enters the National Trust property of New Barton Farm. Spare a glance behind from time to time where successive headlands lead the eye into Cornwall.

The path goes through a kissing gate and enters a more open clifftop area across which it gently descends. From here your way continues ahead on the well-trodden coast path as it gradually bears left, rather than along the less-distinct right fork, although at this point you may wish to drift cautiously towards the cliff edge where you will find a good view of 'The Tomb,' a curious and well-named geological formation on the rocks

The coastline looking back towards Wembury

below. Continue on the coast path as it leads you away from the sea – you will have good river views across Red Cove below, frequently busy with small boats.

Another kissing gate brings you into the area of Warren Point and beyond yet another you'll find yourself beside some rather majestic trees. A further gate brings you to a four-way fingerpost below Rocket Cottage, part of the 19thC coastguard / customs network which operated here and where horse-drawn life-saving apparatus was once stored. A view-rich bench awaits.

Viewpoint below Rocket Cottage

The Mew Stone

This dominant and craggy island in Wembury Bay has a colourful history. In 1744 it became the prison home of a local man who was placed here with his family rather than being transported to Australia. After serving 7 years imprisonment he was 'released' but his daughter elected to stay on the Mew Stone,  where she raised her family. Other residents followed, the last being Sam Wakeman who created a home here for his wife, Ann, whom he married in 1833. The island was the warren for the Langdon Estate and Sam protected their rabbits from poaching, for which service he was allowed to live there rent free, raising pigs and poultry. A magazine of 1934 advised boat trippers to the island to take some snuff for Sam as he had a great fondness for it! He also had a penchant for smuggling which ultimately resulted in his having to leave his rocky home and take up more regular residence on the mainland. In the 1940s the island was bought by the MoD as it was in the firing line of their naval gunnery school, HMS Cambridge, established on the coast at Wembury Point. This land was subsequently put up for sale in 2001 and later purchased by the National Trust. The Mew Stone is now a sea bird sanctuary and visitors are not permitted.

From the fingerpost head right on the coast path towards Warren Point and the seasonal ferry. You are descending now, with views of the Mew Stone to your right which looks particularly picturesque when surrounded by white-sailed yachts. Follow the path to reach an attractive terrace of cottages, passing in front of them – you will see a yellow arrow guiding you at their far end. Beyond here the narrow path winds past gardens to reach Warren Point and the steps to the ferry across Yealm Pool.

The coast path crosses via the ferry but at the top of the steps you bid it goodbye and continue ahead on the footpath which in about 10m swings sharply left up steps, away from the water. It's a bit of a puff up here but attractive views of Newton Ferrers, above the banks of the River Yealm and Newton Creek, should take your mind off the problem. A welcome bench, affording good views over the village and along the creek, offers respite before continuing uphill. The path levels, keep ahead until you reach a three-way fingerpost, from which you need the right-hand option into the wood, signed as an alternative path to Wembury Village via Clitters Wood, 3½ miles.

This woodland path descends steps. Turn left at the bottom, pass through a gate and continue downhill. To your right through the trees you will see the River Yealm. The well-trodden path reaches a fork with a three-way fingerpost. Ignore the "lower loop" path to the right and keep left, signed to Wembury Village, 3 miles. You emerge from the trees to follow the path above the river – look back, there's a not-to-missed view behind you. At another three-way fingerpost, go left, Wembury is now 2½ miles away and you are once more climbing. Two small gates in quick succession lead you into a field where another fingerpost tells you that Wembury is still 2½ miles away. Go slightly left up the field, as directed, to reach another fingerpost at the top of the field. It's still 2½ miles to Wembury! Turn left, following the boundary on your right. At the end of the field gates lead on to a track. Turn right along this, Wembury is now 2 miles away, and follow the track as it swings left. In almost 300m it brings you to another broad crossing track. Turn right along this and follow it to the lane.

At the lane your way lies straight ahead, unless you wish to visit New Barton Farm Shop to the left (closed Saturday afternoon, Sunday and

White sails round The Mew Stone

The River Yealm

Monday). In 250m the lane bends sharp right and you'll see a stepped stile on the left with a metal gate at the top and a raised fingerpost nearby. Go up the steps, admire the edifice of Wembury House on the far side of the ivy-clad wall, then follow the footpath signed for Knighton, ½ mile; the path you need follows the line of the wall as it curves round, keep it to your right and continue ahead when you meet a yellow-arrowed post. At the end of this attractive tree-flanked field a narrow path leads you via old-fashioned metal gates into an area of well-tended allotments, their sheds looking like a rank of miniature beach huts. In the growing season it's a hive of productivity here. Walk ahead between the fenced allotments and continue straight through the field beyond.

At the end of the field a three-way fingerpost points you down steps for Wembury village. At the bottom go left and within 40m go right, now with garden fences on your right. At the road turn left – be careful – keeping to the pavement on the right-hand side. In about 100m you reach The Odd Wheel. Your way now lies sharp right down Traine Road, unless you are first enticed in for refreshment. Follow Traine Road for almost 200m to reach a fingerpost on the left. At the time of writing the finger which should have pointed you left off the lane was missing, but this is the way you need. Cross the stile and set out straight across the field to the far corner. You are now on the Erme-Plym Trail.

At the end of the field go left through the boundary, as directed, and continue through a second field, the houses of Wembury over to your left. When you enter a third field follow the option diagonally left, still on the Erme-Plym Trail and heading towards the sea, visible through a dip in the cliffs. On the far side of the field enter another and bear left, as shown by an arrow, to follow its boundary on your left until a stile takes you into the next field. Cross here and within 40m the path ducks left into the boundary to bring you to another stile. Beyond this a path drops down to an arrowed post. Keep ahead, soon walking down a track between houses. Beyond these you reach a lane on which you turn left uphill.

In 100m you find a two-way fingerpost on the right. Turn right here and follow the track signed towards Church Road, ¼ mile (ignore the rather overgrown path to the left of the broad path). The church eventually comes into view and after slightly more than the ¼ mile you reach a tarmac and concrete drive. Turn right downhill to reach the road at a fingerpost. Cross with care and take the lane opposite heading for Wembury Beach. Within a few metres you find a footpath on the right down some steps. Take this, cross the wooden footbridge and follow the well-trodden path towards the sea. You reach the beach. Go left and wend your way up past the café and toilets to your car park beyond them.

Wembury Beach provides a nice spot to rest at the end of this walk

Other guides from Culm Valley Publishing

An edited collection of beautiful circular walks throughout Devon from a selection of the county's authors and walkers.

Favourite Walks in Devon
ISBN: 978-1-907942-10-5 **£6.99**

The 'Circular Walks' series all contain fifteen walks through the magnificent countryside and coastal terrain of Devon.

Circular Walks in North Devon: including Exmoor
ISBN: 978-1-907942-09-9 **£6.99**

Circular Walks in Central Devon: the walking guide to Mid Devon
ISBN: 978-1-907942-01-3 **£6.99**

Circular Walks in East Devon
ISBN: 978-1-907942-08-2 **£6.99**

The Dozen Dramatic series takes you to the most spectacular scenery each county has to offer. All walks are circular.

A Dozen Dramatic Walks in Cornwall
ISBN: 978-1-907942-03-7 **£5.99**

A Dozen Dramatic Walks in Somerset
ISBN: 978-1-907942-02-0 **£5.99**

A Dozen Dramatic Walks in Dorset
ISBN: 978-1-907942-04-4 **£5.99**

Shortish, circular walks exploring the history (and tea shops!) of Devon and Cornwall's fascinating towns.

Town Walks in Devon
ISBN: 978-1-907942-05-1 **£7.99**

Town Walks in Cornwall
ISBN: 978-1-907942-06-8 **£6.99**

All books available from Culm Valley Publishing: 01884 849085
www.culmvalleypublishing.co.uk / info@culmvalleypublishing.co.uk